An Unexpected Legacy

Strategies of Generosity

G. A. Schupra

An Unexpected Legacy: Strategies of Generosity
By G. A. Schupra

Copyright 2015 by G. A. Schupra

✓ Second printing 8 February 2015

ISBN: 978 1 878559 22 7
Library of Congress Control Number: 2014920969
Saltbox Press
167 Burr Oak Drive
Spring Arbor, Michigan 49283

Price: $20.00

Contents

Introduction

What would you do if a homeless man shows up at your office door, tells you that he has a tax problem, his attorney sent him to see you, and he wants to set up his foundation like Mr. Rockefeller?

That is exactly what happened to me one day while working at our foundation offices in downtown Detroit, Michigan. Throughout the years, I have had the privilege of assisting many individuals, families, and their advisers in distributing accumulated assets to charity. I have also administered and observed the operation of thousands of charitable foundations and endowment funds created over the past century.

These experiences enabled me to identify timeless philanthropic planning principles that anyone who has a desire to help others, or who works with people who want to use their financial resources to benefit charity, should learn and understand.

Not just for individuals who are charitably inclined, the principles presented here are also for the benefit of gift planning professionals, estate and financial advisors, and others who assist clients and donors in establishing legacy gifts to charity.

The story of my encounter with Mr. Howe and the creation of his foundation is true. But I will also share much more about philanthropic planning principles beyond merely the considerations in setting up a charitable foundation. I want to share them in a creative way. Presenting this material in a textbook format would be boring, so you will receive some of this material through the voice of Mr. Howe, my homeless friend. Much of the dialogue between Mr. Howe and me is reconstructed and in many cases hypothetical. However, the principles shared and the stories told are real.

Mr. Howe had a unique personality and was quite elusive throughout my encounter with him. It is my desire that his generosity and care for others be described in a manner that brings him dignity and respect while accurately portraying who he was.

So pull up a chair, prop up your feet, and get ready to meet Mr. Eugene Howe and learn with me the strategies of generosity that he valued and the unexpected legacy he created. Then, maybe you, too, can establish your foundation like Mr. Rockefeller.

Chapter 1
A Foundation like Mr. Rockefeller

I want my foundation to be an endowment!
—Mr. EH

For a homeless man to get to my office on the 20th floor of a large building in downtown Detroit, he would need to get past the security desk in the main lobby, ride the elevator to the 20th floor, and ring the doorbell to have someone from behind a locked door greet him.

No wonder I was startled when our receptionist came into the back copy room in a panic. She frantically exclaimed, "A man is here to see you. He says that his attorney sent him to see you. He has a tax problem and wants to set up his foundation like Mr. Rockefeller!"

"Show him to a seat in the reception area," I said, "and I will be right with him."

This diminutive older man in his 70s had long straggly gray hair down to his shoulders. He wore a gray knit cap. His long trench coat had four pockets down the front of each side. Pieces of paper stuck out of several pockets. Other pockets were bulging with undisclosed contents.

His right pant leg sported a rubber band around his calf area with the hem stuffed into neatly laced high top shoe boots. Over his left pant leg, a long athletic sock pulled up to his knee. The man had a rough gray beard, long curling fingernails, and emitted an unpleasant body odor.

I reached out and shook his hand. His grip was strong and firm, and before I could ask how I might help, he blurted, "My attorney, Mr. Spears, sent me to see you. I have a tax problem and want to set up my foundation like Mr. Rockefeller." Smiling to myself, I invited him into the conference room.

I asked how he had met the attorney, Mr. Spears. He said Mr. Spears prepares his tax return each year at the senior center. Last year he had to pay more tax than usual due to the higher interest he was earning on his certificates of deposit, and he was annoyed that again this year he would have to pay tax on some social security benefits.

Mr. Spears talked to him about charitable gifting to reduce his tax liability and assist organizations that help people who live on the streets of Detroit. Mr. Howe liked that idea. He asked Mr. Spears if he could set up a charitable foundation like Mr. Rockefeller. They discussed various ways to set up his foundation, but ultimately Mr. Spears suggested that he pay a visit to meet with me.

Mr. Howe said he wanted his foundation to grow big. He wanted the interest earned to compound over the years until it reached the size of Mr. Rockefeller's foundation. He did not want any grants paid from his foundation until such time that it grew to that magnitude. Mr. Howe obviously understood the effect of compounding and the growth that results.

He also wanted his foundation to be an endowment. He wanted the foundation to remain in perpetuity with only a small percentage of the foundation assets used each year to support his favorite charitable organizations and activities.

When I showed him a sample foundation agreement, he became irate. "I want my foundation to be an *endowment*! I do not want the principal ever paid! I want it to grow like Mr. Rockefeller's foundation." He did not have much self-control when it came to his emotions. He tended to get emotionally upset. Not threateningly upset, but quite agitated.

Because of the laws, I could not put the endowment language Mr. Howe desired in the agreement, so instead I included the word "endowment" in the name of his foundation. "The Eugene Howe Endowment Fund" sounded satisfactory to Mr. Howe.

I then asked him, "Mr. Howe, what type of charitable organizations and activities do you want your foundation to benefit?"

He contemplated the question for several minutes. He then replied, "I want my foundation to help homeless persons."

I went to my computer and drafted into the charitable purpose clause of the agreement that "The purpose of The Eugene Howe Endowment Fund will be to support charitable organizations and activities that assist homeless persons."

When I read it to Mr. Howe, I thought for sure he was going to jump across the conference room table and grab me. "No, no, no!" he yelled. "I want my foundation to help homeless persons become self-sufficient, independent, contributing members of society!"

"Wow!" I said in a calm voice, hoping to settle his agitation. "That is a tremendous philanthropic vision you have there, Mr. Howe." Mr. Howe just looked off into space through the windows overlooking the bright blue sky and the Detroit River. We had finally captured his vision in writing.

We then stood together and I escorted him to the door. I said I would be in touch with Mr. Spears and we would set up the foundation. Mr. Howe said "fine," opened the door, and briskly left.

When I told Mr. Spears of my encounter with Mr. Howe, he laughed and said, "That sounds just like Eugene!"

I then shared with him the Fund agreement establishing Mr. Howe's foundation. He was pleased and suggested I finalize the draft agreement and have Mr. Howe sign it and send him a copy. I asked, "How will I be able to get in contact with Mr. Howe? I do not have an address or phone number." Mr. Spears replied, "Don't worry, he will be back."

So, I finalized the draft of the donor contribution agreement creating The Eugene Howe Endowment Fund, printed several copies for signing, and then placed my file folder in my credenza behind my desk to wait until Mr. Howe reappeared.

Chapter 2
Meeting Mr. Rockefeller

I committed to learning as much as I could about charitable giving. —Mr. EH

A week later, I had several conference call meetings scheduled. I rushed to my office that Thursday morning trying to get in before I needed to begin my meetings. I took the first call around 9:00 a.m. I answered all of the questions and agreed to send information to the person at the other end. Then, I took the elevator down to the shop in the basement to grab a cup of coffee before my next call at 10:00 a.m.

I purchased my coffee, hopped back on the elevator, and pressed the 20th floor button. It lit up and the elevator began to move, but it stopped on the first floor. The doors opened and who should appear to be getting onto the elevator but Mr. Howe.

He was dressed in the same clothes as the week before. I said, "Good morning, Mr. Howe. How are you today?"

He looked up at me and smiled and said, "I am here to set up my foundation like Mr. Rockefeller."

"Great! Let's go up to my office," I said. We proceeded into the office and I escorted Mr. Howe to the conference room and asked him to wait for me to return. "Can we get you something to drink, Mr. Howe?"

"Yes, I would like a cup of English tea," he replied.

I asked my assistant to contact the 10 a.m. scheduled appointment to reschedule for the afternoon, and to please serve Mr. Howe a cup of English tea. I retrieved Mr. Howe's file from my credenza and then returned to the conference room.

"So, Mr. Howe, I have been in contact with Mr. Spears. We have prepared for you this Fund agreement establishing The Eugene Howe Endowment Fund. It is ready for your signature."

Squinting, Mr. Howe looked up at me. He gave me a wry little smile and said, "It has taken me a long time to get to this point in my life. I have been through many difficult situations. Many people have tried to help me over the years. Some have done it better than others. Now that the time has come for me to sign the piece of paper that will establish my foundation like Mr. Rockefeller, there are many stories that remind me of the things that people did well and the things that people did not realize they were doing. I know they meant well, but sometimes they did not really understand how to help me and others. Before I sign this paper, I want to tell you some of the things people have done that have affected me both good and bad. I will be back next week."

A week later, Mr. Howe reappeared in my office. He said to me, "I have been thinking a lot about all of the times throughout the years that I have encountered people in need and the organizations that assist them."

"Who might you be referring to, Mr. Howe?"

"You know, those organizations that provide services and assistance to people in need. I am also talking about those foundations that give money to help charities."

Mr. Howe continued, "You know, I used to have a lot of money. It was a lot more than I have today. I was trained and educated as an accountant."

"Oh, really? Where did you work?"

Mr. Howe reached into one of the pockets on the right front side of his coat, pulled out nail clippers, and began trimming his fingernails: "After I graduated from college I went to work for an accounting firm in Dearborn, Michigan," he replied. "Our firm did a lot of work for Mr. Ford (Henry Ford II) and members of the Ford family. We also worked closely with the Ford Foundation which Mr. Ford's father and grandfather established in 1936."

"So why do you want to create your charitable foundation like Mr. Rockefeller?"

"You see, in 1953 the Ford Foundation moved its office to New York City. Because I was the accountant assigned to the Foundation, I had to travel to New York to help get the office set up and operating properly."

Mr. Howe clipped a few more fingernails on his right hand. "It is there that I first encountered Mr. Rockefeller. One evening after a long day of work, Mr. Ford and a few of his family members who had come to the city to see our progress invited us to dinner at the upscale Tavern on the Green Restaurant located in Central Park on the upper west side of Manhattan. When the five of us walked into the restaurant, we were escorted to a seating area in the back which was quiet and quaint with beautiful lights throughout the space."

He continued, "As we weaved our way through the restaurant Mr. Ford spotted his friend, Mr. Rockefeller (John Davison Rockefeller Jr.). We all paused while Mr. Ford and Mr. Rockefeller greeted each other. It was at that moment when Mr. Ford introduced each of us that I first met Mr. Rockefeller."

Mr. Howe added gleefully, "When Mr. Rockefeller discovered why we were in town and what we were doing, he asked if he could come by the office the next morning. Mr. Ford quickly agreed."

"So, what happened next?"

"The next morning we arrived at the office bright and early and Mr. Rockefeller was there waiting for us. We all went in and Mr. Rockefeller began telling us stories about his father, John D. Rockefeller, Sr., and how he first created their family's foundation. He also described a number of the generous things he had done with his money.

"Do you know that during his lifetime Mr. Rockefeller (Sr.) made charitable gifts totaling more than $530 million?" Mr. Howe marveled. "Mr. Rockefeller spoke as a truly blessed man but also reflected with great humbleness on the responsibility that he, as well as his father, felt concerning the great wealth that God had bestowed upon them.

"That encounter with Mr. Rockefeller left a lasting impression upon me. I committed to learning as much as I could about charitable giving and non-profit organizations. And I said to myself, no matter how much or how little money I have, I want to do something important with it, just like Mr. Rockefeller."

Mr. Howe then stood up, placed the nail clippers back into his coat pocket, looked at me with his wry smile, and scurried away.

Chapter 3
Mr. Howe Lectures on Philanthropy

There are more financial resources now than ever before in the history of the world. Americans, by far, control a significant portion of it. —Mr. EH

One day the following week Mr. Howe knocked on the office door. The receptionist showed him to the conference room and asked if he would like something to drink. "Yes," he said. "I would like a cup of English tea with milk." She notified me of his arrival and served him the cup of tea with milk.

While there was no pre-arranged meeting time, Mr. Spears had told me that Mr. Howe's time for getting his business completed was every Thursday morning at 10 a.m. When I could, I tried to keep that time open in my schedule, guessing that he may appear.

"Good morning, Mr. Howe," I greeted him. "How are you today?"

Taking a sip of tea, he looked up at me and said, "You know, there are more financial resources now than ever before in the history of the world. I was once among the top 10% of the world's adults who control 85% of the global household wealth. Americans, by far, control a significant portion of the wealth in the world." He took another sip of tea, "It is estimated that the poorest of Americans rank in the top third of the wealthiest in the world.

"People think that corporations make the most charitable contributions. However, it is individual donors who control most of the philanthropic wealth in the United States." He was accurate in his information.

"In 2012, more than $316 billion was given to charitable organizations in the US: 79% from individuals (including bequests), 6% from corporations, and 15% from foundations. Twenty years previously, those numbers were different. At that time, 90% came from individuals, 5% from corporations, and 5% from foundations."

I asked how he accounted for the increase in giving from foundations.

He went on, "Every individual has two pockets of money that they give from. They give current gifts from their disposable income, and they give legacy (long-term or deferred) gifts from their accumulated wealth. In fact, many people are much richer than they realize. They think only of how much money they need to live on each month rather than of their total wealth gathered throughout the years."

"I chimed in. "Yeah, like they forget the value of insurance policies, retirement accounts, automobiles, real estate, and other personal assets."

"Exactly!" he said. "Not everyone has to accumulate wealth at the level of Mr. Rockefeller in order to have an impact on society with the accumulated wealth. For example, over the past 30 years, more individuals have left a portion of their accumulated wealth to charitable *foundations* rather than directly to charitable *organizations.* Since 1980, the number of foundations has increased 242%."

"Yes, I am familiar with that trend," I interjected. "And I have a question. Why do you think more Americans are creating charitable foundations?"

Mr. Howe responded. "Although formal charitable giving is predominantly an American phenomenon, people have assisted each other for thousands of years. Persons living in 17th century Great Britain used a unique method of leaving some of their resources to assist others in need.

"In Suffolk, England, between 1620 and 1630, according to a report I read, people viewed their bequests to charity in a disciplined and methodical manner. The first thing they did in preparing their last will and testament was to bequeath their souls to God before dividing their goods. This made them right with God. It also gave them a spiritual perspective that all that they own is God's and helped them make distribution decisions.

"During that time, the average person left gifts to more than four people outside of his immediate family (a measure of one's social circle). Individuals were given charitable bequests, 'the actual poor,' rather than to institutions like here in America. In that era, compassion was the motivation for giving because there were no benefits in the tax code for such charity.

"In addition," he continued, "it was a right rather than an obligation to write one's will. Will-writing was a part of the act of dying during an individual's final stages of illness. This made it easier to discern how much would be available to distribute to heirs."

Passionately he exclaimed, "A study was done reviewing last will and testaments drafted between 1620 and 1630. Do you know what they found? About one quarter of the 1300 wills reviewed in the study left gifts to the poor, primarily in the parish/local community where the individual writing the will owned land!

"A century earlier, King Henry VIII dissolved all of the monasteries that took care of the poor. As a result, Queen Elizabeth enacted the 'Poor Law of 1597/1601' to set up overseers of the poor. These overseers were to collect revenue and distribute funds to the needy. They also helped the recipients find work. To ensure the truly needy were helped, a key aspect of this system was to administer it locally. As one would expect, the rich generally made most of the bequests to the poor. However, a large percentage of the middle class also left charitable bequests."

"I remember reading about that in school," I said.

"You see," Mr. Howe continued, "society has changed significantly over the past 400 years. Yet, there still lives in the human spirit a desire to help those in need throughout the world. For example, governments, non-government organizations, private firms, and charities implement many 'social safety net' programs in order to assist the poor and those most vulnerable. These programs provide cash transfers, food, school supplies, and uniforms, price subsidies for essentials such as food, electricity or public transport, water and utilities, and fee waivers for health care and education. But now we rely on institutions to provide that support rather than individuals helping each other."

Continuing, Mr. Howe said, "In my younger years, I was able to travel to Kenya, Africa, and experience a safari in the Masai Mara. There I discovered that in many communities in Africa, for the sole purpose of helping one another, a social network is developed."

"Oh, really?" I said. "Tell me, how does the social network operate, Mr. Howe?"

Getting a bit nervous, Mr. Howe reached into his coat pocket with his left hand, pulled out a nail file, and began filing his fingernails. Looking me straight in the eye he said, "Well, it's nothing formal. There is no written contract or agreement. Say that you met someone at work. You hit it off and got along with them. You went to dinner and exchanged email addresses. You have formed an informal bond of friendship. As a result, you are in each other's social network. So then, if you are out of work, or your family needs health care assistance or support for other basic needs, you call on your network and each person has an obligation to assist you."

I inquired, "Is that why it is so hard for people in those societies to save money?"

"Exactly!" Mr. Howe exclaimed. "Each person has an obligation to support the needs of those in the social network. The needs are always greater than the resources. The larger the social network, the better the safety net. But the governments of many

African countries do not have the resources to provide the food-and-shelter safety nets that exist in other parts of the world. That's why so many Africans take personal responsibility for each other."

Mr. Howe continued filing each nail on both of his hands as he said, "The same philanthropic, giving spirit exists in Western cultures as well. People in the United States for example, have a great desire to assist those in need. A recent study by U.S. Trust identified the top six reasons why wealthy people give away money." Here Mr. Howe lifted a different unfiled finger as he counted off the reasons:

- Being passionate about a cause
- Having a strong desire to provide others the same opportunity for success they enjoyed
- Longing to have a positive impact on society and the world
- Hoping to encourage charitable giving by the next generation
- Responding to religious or spiritual motivations
- Sensing that they have an obligation to give back to a system that permitted them to accumulate the wealth they have.

Mr. Howe leaned forward and informed me in a confidential manner, "The report also revealed other motives. A lot of people simply want to reduce their tax burden, fulfill a religious or spiritual need, or create a family legacy."

He intensely continued, "This is an interesting contrast. Advisors generally emphasize the tax savings and more complex vehicles for giving when in reality, many clients simply feel the need to be responsible with the wealth with which they have been entrusted. Proper stewardship of resources by future generations is often more important to wealthy individuals than perpetuating the family name and legacy."

"That is very interesting, Mr. Howe," I replied. "As an accountant, you worked with many people and their wealth. What would you say is their number one concern about leaving their wealth?"

Mr. Howe pondered the question, having placed the nail file back in his coat pocket and now stroking his chin with the thumb and index finger of his right hand.

"Well," he said. "A high percentage of wealthy individuals are concerned that their funds are handled properly and not abused by either future generations of their families or by charitable organizations. They want to make sure that wherever they leave their money, the funds will be properly cared for and used in a manner consistent with their values, visions, and goals.

"If everyone, no matter how much or little resources they own, had Mr. Rockefeller's desire to provide for others, communities throughout the world would have all of the resources needed to provide the safety net and quality of life that many desire."

Continuing his reflection, Mr. Howe observed, "Ever since the first moment that Mr. Ford introduced me to Mr. Rockefeller at Tavern on the

Green Restaurant that evening in 1953, I have had great respect for Mr. Rockefeller and his family.

"In order to gain a greater sense of appreciation for what they have accomplished, we need to go back to the beginning and explore what situations occurred and how they approached their philanthropy." Mr. Howe then shared with me a little bit about the history of the Rockefeller Foundation as summarized below.

Philanthropy for 100 years

The philanthropic considerations John D. Rockefeller contemplated in early 20th century are equally significant today. For the past 100 years, the Rockefeller Foundation made grants to assist in making the world a better place to live and raise families.

At the dawn of the 20th century, John D. Rockefeller was the richest man in the world. In the 40 years from his first job as a 16-year-old assistant bookkeeper in 1855 to his unofficial retirement as the head of Standard Oil in 1895, Rockefeller amassed a personal fortune and transformed American business practices. Even after his retirement, thanks to the oil shares he still owned and the demand for gasoline for newly invented automobiles, by 1913 Rockefeller's fortune ballooned even further, amounting to roughly one billion dollars. He chartered the Rockefeller Foundation at this time.

Rockefeller was an ardent, lifelong Baptist, and in keeping with the tenets of his faith, he committed himself to charitable giving as soon as he had any money to give. He said, "From the beginning, I was trained to work, to save, and to give." [1] But by the 1890s, the sheer size of his fortune turned the process of giving into an impossible chore as he attempted to respond personally to thousands of individual appeals.

Making Benevolence a Business

"Did you know that Mr. Rockefeller wanted to be a minister?" Mr. Howe inquired.

"Really?" I replied. "That is fascinating."

"Yeah, but he entered the business world instead, working as a bookkeeper. He made $25 per month and immediately began the practice of donating one tenth of his salary to the church while also teaching Sunday school."

"That helps explain his interest in philanthropy," I mused.

"Interest is one thing," said Mr. Howe. "Knowing how to do it intelligently is another. Once Mr. Rockefeller had the resources to give in a big way, he needed help. Two men stepped in to help Mr. Rockefeller re-envision his ad hoc charity."

"Who were these two men?"

"Frederick T. Gates and Mr. Rockefeller's only son, John D. Rockefeller, Jr. (JDR Jr.), worked with him to promote the development of large-scale philanthropy. They remade personal charity into an organized, institutional enterprise modeled on corporate business practices. This new philanthropy did not seek to provide direct relief to the diseased or impoverished, but instead it looked to systematic, scientific principles to cure the root causes of physical illness and social problems.

"As Gates recalled later, 'I gradually developed and introduced into all his charities the principle of scientific giving, and he found himself in no long time, laying aside retail giving almost wholly, and entering safely and pleasurably into the field of wholesale philanthropy.'[2]

"So you see," injected Mr. Howe, "as Mr. Rockefeller discovered, sometimes it may be better to give funds to an institution that is providing the assistance to persons as compared to trying to assist those individuals directly."

Progressive Era Values

The new ethos of the Progressive Era permeated this "wholesale" philanthropy. Ironically, this new standard evolved in response to the cataclysmic social changes brought about by the large-scale industrial capitalism that Rockefeller himself helped to invent. Although infused into this progressivism were Protestant religious values, it also embraced secular methods, particularly the rationality of science, and the quantitative analysis of the social sciences. Its essential tools were organization, data gathering, education, and demonstration – all techniques the new Rockefeller Foundation would zealously adopt.

Mr. Howe explained, "You know, Mr. Rockefeller's approach was correct. It is not good enough to be able to do the work at hand. You need to be able to do it in an organized manner so that you can continue efficiently in your work and accomplish more in the same amount of time. When I was working at the accounting firm, successfully completing our tasks in the least amount of time required us to approach them in an organized manner. This enabled us to accomplish more while providing greater returns for our efforts."

"Precisely!" I said, smiling inwardly as I realized I was starting to talk like him. "Gathering data is equally important. By collecting, recording, and studying data at your accounting firm, you were able to use the information to make better, informed decisions. Mr. Rockefeller knew that education also was important. Learning more about the information enabled you to further succeed at what you were attempting to accomplish."

"Absolutely correct," Mr. Howe responded. "The quick and unprecedented rise of industrial capitalism created both a vast underclass of unskilled workers and a new middle class that was educated, confident, and cosmopolitan. The professionalized middle class was increasing by the time of the founding of the Rockefeller Foundation.

"Industrial capitalism believed in the power of trained experts and created new systems of credentials in many fields. These degrees included Baccalaureate degrees (4-year), Associate's degrees (2-year), Master's degrees (1st year above Baccalaureate), Specialist degrees, and Doctorate degrees (the highest degree awarded in most fields of study). They also included Certificates of Training in particular fields or trades such as building and construction, health-care, legal affairs, ministry, arts and creative-cultural management.

"The attention industrial capitalism paid to social ills aimed to offset the worst effects of big business while whole-heartedly accepting capitalism. The professional class that would shape the Rockefeller Foundation's new style of philanthropy aimed to apply the scientific, technical, and organizational solutions born of industrial capitalism to public problems."

I listened in amazement to Mr. Howe as he presented this lesson on the history of philanthropy, and I thought to myself, "you never know what homeless people may be thinking about."

Frederick T. Gates Takes the Helm

I learned from Mr. Howe that Rockefeller first met Frederick T. Gates in 1888 when Gates, an ordained minister, was serving as the head of the American Baptist Education Society. Gates and others were working to convince Rockefeller to fund the creation of the University of Chicago, a gift that would eventually transform a defunct Baptist college into a modern, world class university. Impressed with Gates' abilities in business and philanthropy, Rockefeller hired Gates as his full-time personal philanthropic adviser in 1892. Later, Rockefeller credited Gates with being "the guiding genius in all our giving."[3]

"That is one characteristic that I really like about Mr. Rockefeller," stated a passionate Mr. Howe.

"Many wealthy people are convinced that because they are good at making money, they are good at giving it away, and as a result they do not seek the assistance of others. Mr. Rockefeller understood his need for assistance from others who have more experience in the world of charitable giving."

"That is probably also why he was so successful at making money," I added.

Mr. Howe looked at me meaningfully for a long moment. Then he said, "Yes. And that is why I am now hoping to include you in setting up my endowment. You are a younger man than I, and you have abilities that I lack. So I want to be like Mr. Rockefeller in this way as well. He did not try to do it on his own. He relied on the strengths and abilities of others to assist him."

Moved by his confidence in me, I sat in stunned silence and absorbed the wisdom, kindness, and vulnerability this gentleman possessed.

When Mr. Howe saw that I fully understood what he had just confided, he resumed his narrative: "Gates moved quickly to consolidate Rockefeller's haphazard gifts and began to develop the concepts that would guide his designs for all of the Rockefeller philanthropies: efficiency and a centralized system for the distribution of funds.

"The first institution founded in 1901 by Rockefeller that bore his name was the Rockefeller Institute for Medical Research (RIMR). On a vacation in 1897, Gates read William Osler's thousand-page volume *Principles and Practice of Medicine*, published in 1891. He concluded from it that the state of U.S.

31

medicine—and, hence disease control—was sadly lagging. Gates envisioned "qualified men" being amply paid, conducting uninterrupted scientific research at a permanent institution. The Institute, renamed The Rockefeller University in 1965, would become one of the pre-eminent centers of medical research worldwide and the site of major scientific breakthroughs."

"That place is amazing," I exclaimed.

"It certainly is," he agreed. "Do you know that the Rockefeller University has the highest number of Nobel Prizes (24) in relation to personnel involved in research in the world? The researchers at the University perform work in biochemistry, structural biology, molecular cell and developmental biology, medical sciences and human genetics, immunology, virology, microbiology, physics and mathematical biology, and neuroscience."

He further exclaimed, "Do you know that they first identified many important scientific research breakthroughs? For example, they developed the first antibiotic. They also identified the phenomenon of the autoimmune disease and developed tissue culture techniques. Researchers at the University developed the practice of travel vaccination and were the first to culture the infectious agent associated with syphilis. And to top it off, they developed methadone treatment of heroin addiction, devised the AIDS drug cocktail, and identified the appetite-regulating hormone leptin, to name a few!"

I mused aloud, "It goes to show you what can be accomplished when concentrating your resources to achieve an important mission and purpose."

"That's right," Mr. Howe stated. "Three themes evident in the Rockefeller Institute for Medical Research pervaded the Rockefeller philanthropies for most of the 20th century: the commitment to open-ended scientific research, the idea that research values are universal, and the conviction that disease is the root of all other ills—physical, economic, mental, moral, and social."

Predecessors in Education and in Health

Mr. Howe was clearly well versed on the giving strategies of Mr. Rockefeller. He informed me that JDR Jr. joined his father's staff in 1897, but soon found that business was neither his passion nor his talent. His passion and talent was to give money away intelligently. The mark he made would instead be in developing the philanthropic side of the Rockefeller enterprises. Between 1900 and 1910, JDR Jr. and Gates both urged Rockefeller to create a series of "great, corporate philanthropies." Many plans were proposed and discarded as the blueprint for what would ultimately become the Rockefeller Foundation slowly took shape.

JDR Jr's first work in organized philanthropy came about as the result of a 1900 train tour organized by Robert C. Ogden and focused on African American education in the South. Impressed by what he saw at institutions including Hampton and Tuskegee, but dismayed by the lack of any other educational infrastructure, JDR Jr. encouraged his father to create the General Education Board (GEB) in 1903.

While aiming ultimately to increase educational opportunity for African Americans, the GEB quickly saw that to make such improvements it needed to include southern whites in the program. Therefore, it set out to strengthen education "without distinction of sex, race, or creed."[4]

The GEB exemplifies the Rockefeller enterprises' concern with "root causes." Although it aimed to improve education, it recognized that Southern farmers would be more inclined to support better schools if their livelihoods improved. In 1906, the GEB launched a wide-ranging and successful farm demonstration program. In 1909, the GEB recognized that hookworm disease, rampant throughout the South, was a serious obstacle to both education and productive farming. Rockefeller established the Rockefeller Sanitary Commission (RSC) to eradicate hookworm through education, demonstration, and direct treatment.

"You know, that Mr. Rockefeller had to be really smart!" I stated "He understood how to structure his philanthropic goals so that many people had something to gain from their achievement."

"He sure was," replied Mr. Howe. Two predecessor philanthropies were set in place that would become the Rockefeller Foundation's fundamental methods: demonstration programs and infrastructure enhancement. The GEB demonstration program enabled the U.S. Department of Agriculture to establish a comprehensive system of county extension agents that long outlasted the direct involvement of the GEB. Likewise, the Rockefeller Sanitary Commission's campaign to eradicate hookworm disease helped instigate a county-based public health system in the U.S. that could take on other diseases. Repeatedly, the Rockefeller Foundation would continue the basic approaches honed by the GEB and RSC, establishing demonstration programs and using them to develop naturally designed models that extended beyond the original problem."

Mr. Howe paused for breath, then continued, "I love that about Mr. Rockefeller. To address many needs, he developed model programs that demonstrated success in one particular situation. To sustain the model, he then invested in building the infrastructure. How ingenious!

"With this philanthropic philosophy, Mr. Rockefeller created the University of Chicago, making gifts to the institution totaling $35 million over his lifetime," stated Mr. Howe. "Many conclude that with all that he accomplished through his generosity, Mr. Rockefeller must rank as the greatest philanthropist in American history."

Mr. Howe said the positive results of the Rockefeller Institute for Medical Research, General Education Board, and Rockefeller Sanitary Commission reinforced to Rockefeller the benefits of conducting philanthropic business on a large scale. These philanthropies also confirmed the effectiveness of entrusting the disposal of funds to a professional staff governed by independent boards of trustees. In 1907, Rockefeller, Gates, JDR Jr., and family attorney Starr J. Murphy embarked on plans to launch an even broader, more general-purpose organization for giving. As they moved to obtain a corporate charter for this new Rockefeller Foundation, they anticipated little trouble. However, the political winds shifted, and establishing the charter was much harder than anyone anticipated.

"What political winds?" I wondered.

Mr. Howe winked, straightened his shoulders, and said, "Well, Sir. Mr. Rockefeller wasn't always that generous. He did not have a very good reputation due to his business practices. That was spotlighted by a woman named Ida Tarbell."

Along Comes Ida Tarbell

By the early 1900s, John D. Rockefeller, Sr. had finished building his oil empire. For 30 years he had applied his uncanny shrewdness, thorough intelligence, and patient vision to the creation of an industrial organization without parallel in the world. The new century found him facing his most formidable rival ever—not another businessman, but a 45-year-old woman determined to prove that Standard Oil had never played fair. The result, Ida Tarbell's magazine series "The History of the Standard Oil Company," would not only change the history of journalism, but also the fate of Rockefeller's empire, shaken by the powerful pen of its most relentless observer.

Born in a log home in Hatch Hollow, northwestern Pennsylvania, on 5 November 1857, Ida Minerva Tarbell grew up amid the derricks of the Oil Region. Her father, Frank Tarbell, built wooden oil storage tanks and later became an oil producer and refiner. "Things were going well in father's business," she would write years later. "There was ease such as we had never known; luxuries we had never heard of. ...Then suddenly [our] gay, prosperous town received a blow between the eyes."

The 1872 South Improvement scheme, a hidden agreement between the railroads and refiners led by John D. Rockefeller, hit the Pennsylvania Oil Region like a tidal wave. It hit the Tarbells too, leaving behind painful memories that would be rekindled 30 years later. "Out of the alarm and bitterness and confusion, I gathered from my father's talk a conviction to which I still hold—that what had been undertaken was wrong."

"I know Mr. Rockefeller made some business decisions that hurt many people," stated Mr. Howe. "Some of his business dealings hurt many families including Ida Tarbell's."

After graduating from Allegheny College, the sole woman in the class of 1880, Tarbell moved to Ohio to teach science, but resigned after two years. She would find her true calling just months later back in Meadville, Pennsylvania, when she met the editor of a small magazine, *The Chautauquan*. Tarbell's inquisitive mind and her determination to have a career pushed her to become intensely invested in her writing and research projects. At 34, fascinated by the story of Madame Roland, the leader of an influential salon during the French Revolution, she moved to Paris to write her biography.

Ida Tarbell supported herself by writing numerous articles on the City of Light for the popular magazines of the day. This work got the attention of editor Samuel Sidney McClure who was looking for writers for his new monthly magazine. He hired Tarbell as an editor in 1894, and she became *McClure's Magazine's* most successful writer when her series on Abraham Lincoln nearly doubled the circulation of the magazine. Another serialized biography followed, this time on Napoleon, establishing her as a gifted historical writer and an insightful judge of character.

However, events and trends more immediate were calling for attention. The rapidly changing economic landscape and the rise of monopolistic trusts was "disturbing and confusing people," wrote Tarbell. A new generation of investigative journalists, later dubbed "muckrakers" by President Theodore Roosevelt, had set out to wage a campaign to expose corruption in business and political lawlessness. Tarbell latched onto the idea of using the story of Standard Oil to illustrate these troubling issues, persuading McClure to agree to a three-part series on the oil trust.

Tarbell's father, fearing that Rockefeller would retaliate against the magazine, advised her not to do it. Yet she dove into the work with a zeal that matched her antagonist. For almost two years, she painstakingly looked through volumes of public records, including court testimony, state and federal reports, and newspaper coverage. From these, she gathered an overwhelming wealth of information on Rockefeller's ascent and the methods used by Standard Oil. The breadth of her research was remarkable, but even more impressive was her ability to digest Rockefeller's complicated business maneuvers into a narrative that would be accessible and engaging to the average reader.

"Ida Tarbell must have been relentless," I observed. "It appears that she did not leave one stone unturned in her research on Mr. Rockefeller and his business practices. And she was fair in her assessments."

"I think you are correct in your observation," responded Mr. Howe. "Although always modest about her prose, Tarbell was an eloquent writer, able to combine her keen analytical skills with a sense of drama."

Ida Tarbell wrote in July of 1903, "Now, it takes time to secure and to keep that which the public has decided it is not for the general good that you have. It takes time and caution to perfect anything which must be concealed. It takes time to crush men who are pursuing legitimate trade. However, one of Mr. Rockefeller's most impressive characteristics is patience. There never was a more patient man, or one who could dare more while he waited.... He was a general who, besieging a city surrounded by fortified hills, viewed from a balloon the entire great field, observed how to take this point, reach this hill, and command this fort. Nothing was too small: the corner grocery in Browntown, the humble refining still on Oil Creek, the shortest private pipeline. Nothing, for little things grow."

"Ida Tarbell did have it right about Mr. Rockefeller," Mr. Howe told me. "He was ruthless in his business practices and did not have regard for other competition. His goal was to remove all competition as quickly as he could."

Instantly popular with McClure's readers, "The History of the Standard Oil Company" grew to be a 19-part series, published between November 1902 and October 1904. Tarbell wrote a detailed exposé of Rockefeller's unethical tactics, sympathetically portraying the plight of Pennsylvania's independent oil workers.

Still, she was careful to acknowledge Rockefeller's brilliance and the flawlessness of the business structure he had created. She did not condemn capitalism itself, but "the open disregard of decent ethical business practices by capitalists." About Standard Oil, she wrote, "They had never played fair, and that ruined their greatness for me."

Tarbell capped the series with a two-part character study that revealed her fixation with the man she had been studying for the better part of five years. Focusing on Rockefeller's weary appearance, she called him "the oldest man in the world—a living mummy," and accused him of being "money-mad" and "a hypocrite." "Our national life is on every side distinctly poorer, uglier, meaner, for the kind of influence he exercises," she concluded. Deeply hurt by this last attack from "that poisonous woman," as he called her, Rockefeller refused to engage in any public rebuttal of her allegations. "Not a word," he told his advisors. "Not a word about that misguided woman."

Hailed as a landmark in the history of investigative journalism, "The History of the Standard Oil Company" is the most comprehensive study of the building of Rockefeller's oil empire. In 1999 it was listed number five among the top 100 works of 20th-century American journalism.

Having become one of the most influential women in the country, Ida Tarbell nevertheless opposed the suffrage movement, arguing that women's rights advocates belittled traditional female roles and that women's contributions belonged in the private sphere. She died of pneumonia in 1944 at the age of 86.

"I have to hand it to Ida Tarbell," mused Mr. Howe. "She sure gave it to Mr. Rockefeller in a most professional manner. Her work is one of the reasons that Mr. Rockefeller set up his foundation. He wanted to show the public that he was a good person and cared about people. At first, Ms. Tarbell and others were cynical about the foundation, which is why there was political opposition to its founding. However, over time Mr. Rockefeller's generosity went above and beyond the expectation of his critics— even Ida Tarbell was ultimately impressed—leading most people to rank him as one of the top philanthropists in American history. It goes to show you that regardless of your motivation for being generous, the act of kindness is truly contagious," exclaimed Mr. Howe.

He continued, "Like Mr. Rockefeller and the British citizens of the17th century, if every one of us set aside a portion of our wealth to benefit our communities, the impact could be incredible. To see evidence of such potential impact, all that you need to do is to look at the cities and towns around the country whose forefathers set aside a portion of their wealth to benefit the community throughout the generations."

"I agree," said. "Just look around you. Look at the names on the buildings and institutions of all kinds: Art museums, public libraries, educational institutions, hospitals carry the names of Carnegie, Ford, Kresge, Kellogg, and Mellon to name a few."

"Precisely," he snapped. "The quality of life and services now available in those communities are significantly better than in communities whose forefathers did not set aside resources for future community benefit. That is why I want to do my part and set up my foundation like Mr. Rockefeller."

Chapter 4
Discover Your Philanthropic Passion

Charitable foundations continue to benefit communities through the generations. —Mr. EH

Mr. Howe was correct in thinking he had enough money to establish a foundation. In 2011, the Internal Revenue Service recorded the existence of more than one million charitable organizations. Religious congregations made up 322,485 (one third) of them. In 2012, the greatest percentage of wealthy households gave charitable contributions to organizations serving needs in the following areas:

> 80% of wealthy households contributed to educational institutions
>
> 79% contributed to organizations meeting basic needs
>
> 69% gave to arts and cultural institutions
>
> 65% contributed to health related organizations
>
> 65% assisted religious organizations

Mr. Howe said that when establishing philanthropic goals, you should look to areas of personal interest including vocation, hobbies, community services, and support activities. You can also consider providing help with family member issues such as special needs, mental illness, domestic violence and abuse, drug and alcohol dependency, and other addictions.

Then you can identify charitable organizations that serve in those areas. For example, if you want to benefit an organization that helps people with basic needs, the Salvation Army may be for you. If you would like to provide job training assistance for individuals with special needs, then Goodwill Industries is the type of organization you may find attractive.

With the information so readily available on the Internet today, you can easily gather all types of information on charitable organizations doing a particular kind of work. Websites of recommended organizations you can easily access include Guide Star, the Foundation Center, Internal Revenue Service, Charity Watch, and the websites of organizations themselves.

Volunteering is one of the most effective ways to research an institution. Opportunities vary based on the specific mission and purpose. You can become acquainted with an institution by attending special events, meeting with organization members, and talking with people served by them. Interviewing governing board members also fosters a better sense and understanding of the organization's capabilities.

How to Give

Mr. Howe was very methodical in his approach to giving. He said that after you have made a list of the organizations you would like to help, the next step is determining how to give your money.

Detailing areas of interest you may wish to benefit can help as well. These include the geographic location of the charity or the purpose for which it exists. When creating a foundation, identifying areas of interest may be more helpful over a longer period.

"I once had a client who managed a charitable trust that was established to support a specific area of interest in a particular geographic region," Mr. Howe said, reaching his right hand into the lower middle pocket on the right side of his coat to pull out a package of red licorice. He took a bite and said as he chewed, "The Dewitt C. Holbrook Memorial Trust is a great example of how a charitable foundation can continue to help a community throughout many decades."

As he chewed the red licorice, he told of the Dewitt C. Holbrook Memorial Trust, a charitable foundation established in 1929. "The trust supports legal education and training throughout the Wayne County metro-Detroit area," he explained.

"Holbrook's daughter, May Walker, who wished to honor her father, a well-respected lawyer from Monroe, New York, established the trust with $10,000. After Holbrook moved to Michigan in 1832, he served as a major in the Blackhawk War, studied law in Detroit, and became county clerk. Holbrook died in 1892.

"Throughout the years, the foundation has seen prudent management while each year giving away the income to deserving charities providing legal education and training in the city of Detroit and Wayne County. The foundation now grants $100,000 per year, an amount 10 times the original bequest. Through this foundation—now valued at about two million dollars—Holbrook and his daughter are still making an impact in Detroit.

"What's amazing to me about that Holbrook Foundation is that it was established eight months before the '29 market crash," I exclaimed.

"How true," replied Mr. Howe as he picked a speck of licorice from between his teeth. He concluded, "It has continued to grow in value through the years while at the same time supporting the interests of Mr. Holbrook and his daughter. What a great tribute to them and example of how a foundation is supposed to work!"

Make the List

Mr. Howe was a list maker, so it didn't surprise me when he told me this: "After identifying specific charities, list the reasons you want to benefit them. This exercise is especially important in documenting, for posterity, your specific donor intent and motivation.

"When I sat down to identify the types of charitable organizations that I want my foundation to support, I thought about all of those days living on the streets of Detroit. I was often cold, hungry, wet, and tired. I saw other persons living on the streets and tried to do my best to help them. Once I received an extra blanket and shared it with another homeless person. And when I came across more food than I could eat, I would 'break bread' with my street friends. So assisting with the basic needs of homeless persons is very important to me.

"But meeting the basic needs is not enough! Of course I want my foundation to support charitable organizations and activities that meet the basic needs—but I want my foundation to do more. Every day on the streets I thought about my days at the accounting firm and how thankful I was to have a job skill and blessed to have received an education and training that allowed me to work. I would say to myself that I want to create a foundation that will help these people become self-sufficient, independent, contributing members of society.

"You know," I added, "It may be useful to review a roster of opportunities provided by the organization relative to their long-term financial needs. These opportunities can include such things as endowed programs, projects, educational scholarships, research endowments, and endowed 'chairs' at universities."

Mr. Howe knew that most charity organizations do an excellent job of explaining why donors should support current needs with disposable income. However, they are not nearly as good at presenting their need for lasting resources from estate gifts. Instead of mentioning particular long-term support opportunities, the charities often focus their message on payment methods.

He was clearly annoyed by this short-sighted thinking and said, "Always ask an organization for its list of giving opportunities. If you don't ask, it's like a person going into a store and, before he has a chance to look at the merchandise, the sales clerk asks, 'Will you be paying with MasterCard, Visa, or personal check?'

"That is what charitable organizations do when they ask you to consider putting them in your estate plan or designating them to be a beneficiary of a retirement plan, life insurance contract, or charitable income trust. They should first provide a roster of long-term financial needs."

Mr. Howe believed these organizations needed to focus on the end-result charitable purpose, and I supplied him with an illustration for his point. I said, "When I go into a restaurant, the people there know I am hungry and are coming in to get something to eat. So why don't they simply ask, 'What do you want to eat?' They don't do that! Instead, they provide a menu offering various meals with descriptions of what I can expect and how much it will cost.

"Through the menu and the daily specials, they are attempting to drive buying decisions. They are focusing on what they can offer and how much it will cost. They highlight the 'end result' of my experience rather than the payment methods. Also, if I see something on the menu I would like to change, the restaurant will often accommodate my request."

"Your story makes perfect sense to me," Mr. Howe said. "In the same way, when charitable organizations do not offer a giving menu to help guide your estate plan, they will not thrive in this area. If they fail to point out long-term financial priorities, how likely are they to carry out your instructions with the money you give them? If the organization does not have such policies, or has not established a formal management process for the stewardship of your gifts, then you should think twice about giving to that organization."

"What would you do instead?" I wondered.

He said, "When that's the case, you may want to create your own organization able to achieve your vision—just like Mr. Rockefeller!" He reminded me of how Mr. Rockefeller established the University of Chicago and then continued to opine by telling me another story of generosity:

"Helen Kay was an executive secretary working in the automotive industry. Over time, she accumulated a great deal of automotive stock. With her attorney's help, she created the Helen Kay Charitable Trust. She had three purposes for her foundation. First, she named charities that she cared deeply about and provided annual support during her lifetime as well as perpetual yearly support from her trust after her death.

"Second, Ms. Kay gave to organizations which carried out cancer and heart research. She believed that the more we can learn about cancer and heart disease, the better quality of life the medical community will be able to provide for humankind.

"The third thing she did was to designate money for community support in both southeast Michigan and western Pennsylvania. She grew up in western Pennsylvania and was a big Steelers football fan, yet she lived most of her life in southeast Michigan, so it made sense that she would want to improve the two communities she loved."

Excited by my interest in his story, Mr. Howe dipped into his accountant's memory and offered me some numbers: "Over time, the foundation assets grew to more than seven million dollars, generating an annual grant budget of around $350,000."

Each year, institutions from the foundation's three designated areas of interest apply to Ms. Kay's Trust for support. For example, one grant from her foundation helped establish a produce market in Detroit recognized as a national and state model for providing healthy food choices to urban communities.

"Because of the vision of people like Mr. Rockefeller and Ms. Kay," Mr. Howe emphasized, "they created charitable foundations that continue to benefit communities through the generations."

Chapter 5
Venture Philanthropy

Making a gift to a nonprofit organization is similar to investing in a for-profit business. —Mr. EH

Giving away money is not easy. It actually takes a lot of work if you are to do it in the right way. Mr. Howe was very keen in his observations about giving money to charity. He had much to say on the subject.

"Watching clients give away money during my days as an accountant, I noticed that making a gift to a nonprofit organization is similar to investing in a for-profit business," reflected Mr. Howe as he reached into his coat pocket and pulled out nasal spray. "You must evaluate the value in the product (mission) and see if it aligns with your own values, visions, and goals. You must also evaluate the leadership to determine their ability to deliver on what they say they can do."

Raising his nose toward the sky, he placed the nasal sprayer into his right nostril and gave it a shot. He then proceeded with his reflection about giving away money.

"Many nonprofit organizations talk about their missions and purposes merely in terms of the features and benefits they provide. While those are important, it is more compelling when they are able to measure the impact their services have in our society.

"If you wish to establish a charity, you need to view philanthropic decisions the same way you would any other investment: what is the expected return on the investment for society as a whole?

'A common problem when people give money to charity is that they don't understand the charitable business. They may know how to run a for-profit business and make money, but they do not have experience running a nonprofit organization. My approach, on the other hand, is to work toward understanding the charity and its needs to accomplish the mission and purpose."

"What do you mean, Mr. Howe?" I inquired. "Can you give me an example?"

Raising his nose toward the sky, this time he placed the nasal sprayer into his left nostril and gave it two shots. "Sure," he snorted. "For example, many donors feel that fundraising expenses should not exceed 10% of an organization's operating budget. People also tend to believe that administrative expenses should not be higher than 15-25% of the overall operating budget. Depending on the type of mission, this can be difficult, particularly if individual staff members deliver a significant amount of its services."

I quipped, "A great example is educational institutions where, except for the physical plant and buildings, most expenses incurred are on faculty to teach and staff to administer. Granted, sometimes faculty and staff to student ratios can become out of line and too expensive to operate, but it is hard to judge if the institution is prudent with their resources using a simple percentage formula."

"Exactly!" he said. "The issue becomes cyclical in that to maintain lower administrative costs for donors, institutions may keep salaries very low. As a result, the only way for a charity employee to get a significant pay increase is to change jobs. This job-changing merry-go-round in the nonprofit world has detrimental effects on the industry. It often results in a lack of continuity within an organization. Regulating and running a nonprofit is complex and requires that organizations recruit and retain top-quality talent. When the organization attempts to work off a shoe-string budget, it is challenging to attract qualified personnel...."

"What do you recommend?" I interrupted.

Taking my interruption as a chance to give his right nostril one more shot of the nasal spray, he placed the sprayer back into his coat pocket and answered, "When I would review the books of a nonprofit organization, many times I was appalled and amazed at the same time. I was appalled at the sparse salaries on the one hand, yet amazed at the commitment, dedication, and service that the employees gave in spite of the low compensation.

"To address the talent issue, sometimes a nonprofit will pay a higher salary to secure a qualified person to serve as the executive director, while failing to provide sufficient salaries for the rest of the employees. This may lead to a lack of capability in delivering the services at an adequate level.

"Another way charities attract qualified personnel is by recruiting retiring executives from the corporate world who want to contribute their time to a nonprofit and serve as the executive director. Although they may be willing to work for a lower salary, they do not always view their work as 'full-time' or in it for the 'long-run.' As a result, the organization does not always achieve the expected outcomes it is seeking."

"Mr. Howe," I said, "it sounds like attracting and retaining competent staff is a real challenge in the nonprofit industry."

He glanced down at his grey suede high top shoes and softly commented, "The talent issue in the nonprofit world is troubling to me. Some organizations seek to attract talent to their governing boards and not staff. That is easy, as typically, people will go to work in the for-profit arena, but assist nonprofits by serving as members of the governing boards. Although it is important that top quality persons serve in governance positions, the executive staffs actually execute operations. Without top staff, Board members are not always in a position where they can assist operationally."

"I agree completely," I said. "Philanthropists can help solve this problem by focusing on a holistic approach. That means entrusting more money in order to empower the staff to get the job done. Instead of making charitable decisions based on our own values and our own metrics for measuring these values. We need to be students of philanthropic metrics in order to be good philanthropists."

As I was talking, Mr. Howe was reaching with his right hand into one of his bulging coat pockets from which he pulled out a crumpled bag of peanuts in the shells. "Tiger Stadium Germack Peanuts" read the label. He offered me a peanut and then began shelling one for himself as he said, "I recently read an interview with Bill Gates and Bono. You know, that U2 singer guy, not the Sonny singer!" Mr. Howe chuckled.

"When asked about being a numbers geek, Bono replied, 'I've learned to be an evidence-based activist, to cut through the crap, find out what works and what doesn't work. Repeat what works, increase it, and stop doing what doesn't work. I don't come from a hippie tradition of let's-all-hold-hands and the world's going to be a better place; My thing's much more punk rock.'"

Mr. Howe offered me a second peanut as he continued to report Bono's passionate thoughts: "I enjoy the math, actually. The math is incredible! There are nine million people on AIDS medication. In 2003, there were 50,000. This is the most extraordinary thing. I just want to give thanks to the taxpayers who are paying for that. Because this is a remarkable thing, numbers work.

"In the last ten years, infant mortality is down. I think it's 7,256 fewer deaths a day. That's a decrease from 9.4 million to 7.2 million, something like that. I love these numbers. These are sexy numbers. They rhyme somewhere in my head."

By now, there was a plethora of peanut shells all over and around Mr. Howe's grey suede high-top shoes. "I love that about Bono!" Mr. Howe exclaimed. "As a fellow numbers guy, I can attest that the numbers don't lie. If presented fairly and correctly, they can tell a story."

I asked, "Did you learn anything from Bill Gates in that interview?"

"Yes! He said he's always learning through going on field visits, meeting with scientists, and looking at the numbers; it's a collage of those things that come together. 'For our health work,' Mr. Gates said, 'it's been figuring out how primary health care systems can be really well run—and that gets you the vaccine coverage, it teaches the mother about things to do before birth and after birth, the nutrition things, the reproductive health supplies. It's amazing how some countries spend very little on their primary health care system and they get 95% of the kids vaccinated, and some spend a lot more and get 30% vaccinated.' So every aspect is important: the personnel systems, measurement, training, and hiring."

Mr. Howe then switched to talking about what Mr. Gates learned in working with the U.S. education system when he saw a 10% to 15% improvement with the small schools initiative—which just wasn't enough progress.

"So we got very focused on how teachers get feedback," said Mr. Howe, quoting Mr. Gates: "What are the exemplars doing right? Can you help people improve their personnel system and not just the compensation piece? Because that turns out to be secondary to the idea of professional development, analysis, and measurement. It's obvious now, but it took a lot of time and money to have that be a primary model that we apply."

"Can you put everything I've said to you in a nutshell?" he asked, smiling and glancing around at all the peanut shells.

I said, "It appears that Mr. Bono, Mr. Gates, and Mr. Rockefeller have similar approaches to their giving. These men have taken a lesson from Mr. Rockefeller by focusing their giving on creating a model to solve a specific issue. You can then replicate that model to solve other issues. At the same time, Mr. Gates is investing in the structure of the organizations and systems to make them sustainable."

"Absolutely correct!" responded my teacher. "You get an 'A' for the day." He then took the bag of peanuts, crumpled down the top, and placed the bag back into one of the pockets of his coat. "Do you ever watch television?" he asked.

"Some," I replied.

"Did you see Lesley Stahl on CBS News' 60 Minutes interviewing Howard Buffett, the son of billionaire business executive, Warren Buffett, on his work assisting farmers in Africa?"

"No, but I bet it was worth watching."

"Yes! I was staying in a shelter one night and all of us watched it. In addition to being the successor to his father's Berkshire Hathaway Company, Howard is a corn and soybean farmer in Nebraska and Illinois. He also has a passion and commitment to help alleviate world hunger. Through the Howard G. Buffett Foundation, he provides $50 million per year to assist farmers in Ethiopia, Afghanistan, and all corners of the world.

"He visits as many as 20 countries each year teaching farming methods to farmers. He initially began bringing with him high technology farming equipment, seed, and fertilizer. The problem was that once his initiative was complete, the farmers in Africa, Asia, or elsewhere in the world did not have the resources to sustain the high tech methods. As a result, the initiative ultimately failed.

"We need to change our approach," said Howard. "When working in other countries we need to quit thinking about how we farm in America and, instead of pushing the American system, we need to work with the local farmers to develop better ways that they can farm within their respective resources and systems."

Mr. Howe opined, "I love that about Howard Buffett. Instead of going into these developing countries and thinking that our way is the only way of farming, he is wisely attempting to integrate tried-and-true farming methods within the capacity and capability of the local farmers."

I then shared with Mr. Howe a similar experience from my own travels: "I was traveling in Africa with a small group of people from the U.S. and Canada," I told him. "We were walking through one of the large slums in Nairobi, Kenya, with a local Kenyan man as our guide and protector. The roads were narrow and made of mud with large potholes. Little tent-like shops made from canvas and tree poles lined both sides of the road. Merchandise was displayed on fold up or homemade wooden tables and shelves. All types of items were on display—cooking pots and pans, bed frames and mattresses were all along the road, along with produce such as bunches of carrots, potatoes, and beans. Bags of rice were on the ground under tables and live chickens roosted on the tables waiting for someone to purchase them and take them home for dinner. The aromas of chicken, lamb, and corn roasting on small, charcoal fueled grills filled the air.

"We turned off the road onto an extremely narrow path. A thin stream flowed through the middle of the path and most of the time we straddled the stream as we walked. Children played along the path displaying big smiles, waving and asking us the question, 'How are you,' as a way to practice their English since most spoke Swahili. At the time, we did not realize the stream was part of the sewage system that flowed down into a pool where the women were cleaning clothes. The stench in the air made it hard to breath. In places, it was so strong that I would gag and become nauseated.

"As we walked through the muck of the Mathare slum, we noticed a woman along the road roasting and selling coffee beans. I wondered about the profitability of her business. I asked our Kenyan guide if the woman could sell enough to make a living.

"The guide looked at me and said, 'She is alive.' Then I understood that whether the business supports her living or whether she supports her business, at least she has something to get up in the morning to look toward and something of value to do. Her self-worth and doing something productive in society and in her community is as important as how much money she makes."

Mr. Howe gave me a meaningful look and said, "This is a vital insight. Whatever we pursue, we want to help people do something constructive and to have self-worth while enhancing their society. The metric here is simple: Finding a way to feed and take care of myself today while positively serving my community will bring much self-worth to anyone who tries."

Throughout our exchange of stories I was learning that when deciding to make a grant, the donor often needs to simply take the risk of just saying "yes," even if all of the information is not present or does not line up exactly. Mr. Howe underscored this lesson by saying, "In that interview with Bill Gates, the interviewer asked how he addresses the corruption when working in developing countries. Mr. Gates' reply made the point about not everything lining up exactly as we think it should. He said, 'You should expect up to 5% of your gift might be used for some inappropriate purpose. If you can't handle that fact, then you shouldn't be in the game.'"

Mr. Howe then shared another example of venture philanthropy by describing an extremely generous gift from the wife of someone he called the "hamburger guy." The Joan Kroc estate made a gift to the Salvation Army at the beginning of the 21st century. Mrs. Kroc was the widow of Ray Kroc, founder of the McDonald's Corporation. When she passed away, she left a $1.8 billion bequest. However, her bequest came with restrictions. Her gift was to be used to create community centers in low-income residential areas around the United States modeled after The Salvation Army Ray and Joan Kroc Corps Community Center in San Diego, California.

Consistent with the Salvation Army's mission, these centers were to be holistic in their approach toward the programs they offered to children. Programs provide opportunities that facilitate positive, life-changing experiences through art, athletics, personal development, spiritual discovery, and community service. The Center is to help bridge the gap between potential and opportunity for children and adults, strengthen individuals and families, and enrich the lives of seniors.

"One day Mrs. Kroc toured San Diego," Mr. Howe said as he pulled a bright, shiny, silver, round doorknob out of a coat pocket. "There she recognized a community in desperate need of a safe gathering place, a place with facilities and trained professionals to nurture children's social skills, arts appreciation, and athletic potential. She described the Kroc Center as being a beacon of light and hope in the community. She trusted the Salvation Army to carry out her values in a thoughtful and integral manner."

Tossing the doorknob from hand to hand, he continued: "The idea of replicating the San Diego Kroc Center throughout the country sounded great. However, the broad scope of the programming was more extensive than the Salvation Army had expertise and funds to carry out. Through the bequest, funds were available to build the facilities, but developing a finance plan to sustain the programming was challenging. Planned community center projects were never able to get off the ground due to the lack of resources necessary to support the on-going programming.

"Do you know how long it took for the Salvation Army to accept Mrs. Kroc's bequest?" Mr. Howe asked, now rubbing the smooth and shiny silver knob.

"Probably in a nano-second," I replied.

"Guess again," he said. "Because of the size and scope of the dollars and the restriction to build community centers, it took them four months to decide to accept the gift. The bequest had the potential to affect significantly the Salvation Army's mission, both for good and for bad.

"For example, when the public learned that the Salvation Army was the recipient of a $1.8 billion bequest, it could seriously hinder their continuing ability to raise the usual funds necessary to carry forward their existing mission. The public would think they have plenty of money and no longer need their support. But that was not the case. The bequest funds were restricted to Mrs. Kroc's community center development plan. They could not be used for any other Salvation Army program. Give them credit for not accepting in a nano-second!"

"Come on Mr. Howe. We all know that charities are driven by the almighty dollar," I retorted.

"That proves my point," affirmed Mr. Howe. "It demonstrates Mrs. Kroc's good judgment in trusting her funds with the Salvation Army who were thoughtful and careful in their deliberations to accept such a gift."

"How have they done in setting up the centers?" I asked.

He gleefully responded as he placed the doorknob back in his coat pocket: "The total Kroc gift was $1.8 billion. The Salvation Army has used approximately half for construction and half for endowment to support facility maintenance and programming. The gift has allowed them to create 25 centers in low-income communities throughout the country. Each center averages more than 62,500 square feet and combined currently employ nearly 3,000 people while serving over 110,000 patrons."

I said, "Kudos to Mrs. Kroc and her advisers for their philanthropic risk-taking. What a tremendous impact she continues having on our world as a result of her generosity."

"Well," reflected Mr. Howe, now scratching his chin with his forefinger and thumb. "The risk was not in trusting the Salvation Army with her funds. After all, they are impeccable regarding their integrity in handling people's gifts."

He continued, "The bequest may have been more effective in achieving her ultimate philanthropic goal if her advisors had approached several nonprofit organizations in advance of her passing. It would have allowed the organizations to be much more prepared to accept and implement the restrictions of her bequest. In addition, they could jointly create and operate community centers involving the core

63

competencies of various organizations to help deliver the programming requirements of the gift. The Salvation Army could still serve as the lead organization in the collaboration. And they would have a greater constituency to approach for on-going program support."

"Mr. Howe," I said. "Are you saying that if organizations are able to collaborate, then our charitable giving decisions can be the most effective?"

"Yes," he emphatically replied. "We may have to be more adventurous and creative in our philanthropic decisions. We may need to take more risks with the goal of not only improving society to a greater degree, but also improving the leadership at the organizations who work so hard to advance our civilization."

Chapter 6
When Gifts are Harmful

Many contributors have a longer history with a nonprofit organization than the staff currently working there. —Mr. EH

Charitable giving is an emotionally charged activity. For the giver, there is great satisfaction in doing something good. For the charitable organization, there is great satisfaction in having others join in its cause and mission. However, at times, the emotional connection created between giver and receiver can cause the situation to go awry and harm to occur.

As you can probably tell, Mr. Howe is quite an emotional person. He is passionate, sincere, and thoughtful. For someone who had lived on the streets of Detroit for many years, he amazed me with his knowledge and experience in the world of charitable giving.

Mr. Howe understood that charitable organizations often attempt to create an emotional connection with their donors in order to influence them into making larger contributions than they might otherwise consider. Donors who have a great desire to help an organization typically have experienced something personal with the group and its mission that takes on a special meaning. They may have attended a summer camp that changed their lives. Perhaps they enrolled in an educational institution or were successfully treated at a medical center and the experience positively influenced their lives.

This passion is commendable yet carries with it a specific danger. When making gift decisions while deeply involved, donors will often attempt to impose their own preferences and priorities on the charity through adding restrictions on their gifts. When those gift restrictions conflict with the priorities of the charity, frustration and emotional hurt can occur if the charity does not wish to comply with the gift requirements.

This situation often happens in churches and smaller nonprofit organizations where gifts make up a significant part of the budget. The contributors are actively involved and take a personal interest in the organization's success. They know enough to be thoughtful about their giving, but do not fully understand the direction of the organization.

When a gift with restrictions that favor the donor's perspectives and desires conflicts with the charity's overall direction, the organization is forced to either accept the gift with the restrictions and do something outside of its strategic direction, or turn it down. It is in these situations that emotional pain and hurt feelings can occur.

Mr. Howe correctly observed, "Fundraising professionals understand the emotional connection that they create in trying to get money out of their donors, but they don't always think about the things that are important to the donor. The fundraiser generally focuses on the needs of the charity and ignores the desires of the giver."

"What is a better approach?" I asked him.

He said, "The job of the successful fundraiser is to be the match-maker between the charity's and the donor's goals. It only makes common sense that you listen to the donor and embrace the vision for his gift. You then try to figure out how to match what he wants with what the organization needs. Creating emotional connection certainly influences someone's 'buy-in' with the charity. However, the same emotional connection used to create 'buy-in' also causes people to think about what is important to them about the organization and facilitates gift restriction ideas. If these ideas are ignored, then great emotional hurt can occur."

Here Mr. Howe reminded me of something many charity staff members forget: Many contributors have a longer history with the nonprofit organization than the staff currently working at the charity. The person who graduated from a university 40 years ago will most likely have more institutional memory than the contact person hired by the university five years ago.

Development professionals and nonprofit executives do not always consider this fact when doing their jobs. Meeting current fundraising goals is necessary and they focus on those priorities. They often fail to consider the long-term involvement and commitment of their donors. When long-term contributors begin to express their opinions about the direction of the organization or the fund development priorities, the staff might discount those opinions or ignore their concerns. This can result in great pain for the donors, especially if staff members are aloof in their response.

"I have to tell you," blurted Mr. Howe as he took a pair of scissors from his side pocket, "about a time that a client of mine wanted to give $10 million to endow a department at her alma mater. She desired to provide enough resources to make the department one of the best in the country."

Taking a piece of paper that was poking out of his right coat pocket, he began folding it until it was a small square. He then said, "Her idea was to provide a challenge where she would contribute one dollar to the endowment for the department for every dollar the department raised for any purpose.

"The institution told her that she could give her $10 million to endow the department, but said they would not conduct a fund raising campaign asking the alumni to match the gift. They said they do not solicit alumni for specific departments.

"That's their decision as to how they want to handle their business," he said, while making small snips in the paper square with his scissors. "But what really frosted me is that six weeks after submitting our gift proposal, I had to call the institution to learn of their response to my client.

"This poor response of the institution greatly disappointed my client. She has since passed away, but up to her last days, she would not contribute a penny to that organization. Given how she loved the school because of the tremendous impact it had on her life, it seems tragic that her giving restrictions combined with their ineptitude at responding to her request culminated in a double failure. The school received no funding, and she experienced the pain of not joining in to support the institution she loved."

As he talked, Mr. Howe had cut the paper into a beautiful origami shape. He opened it to show me the design while saying, "Similarly, donors need to be sensitive and respectful of the existing leadership. They need to be understanding and not desire their own interests, instead recognizing the staff's abilities and expertise in their respective fields. Imposing gifting priorities and restrictions without regard for the organization's financing priorities can be equally painful to the staff of the charity.

"However, when a nonprofit fails to identify its long-term financing plan and needs, donors begin to develop their own priorities for the organization through various gift restrictions.

"I can tell you many situations where my clients placed restrictions on their estate gifts because the charity failed to identify their own priorities," said Mr. Howe. "Take, for example, a nonprofit executive who approached a consulting professional and indicated that she had a problem on her hands. One of her donors, who was 80-years-old, was in the process of fine-tuning his estate plan."

"What was the problem?"

"In his estate plan, he named the organization to receive more than a million dollars upon his death. However, he restricted his gift to endow three new programs that the nonprofit executive indicated were not needed and obsolete. Further, the million dollars was nowhere near enough to annually pay for the programs. In order to accept the gift, the organization would need to create three unnecessary programs and raise the funds each year to operate them."

I blurted, "What did the consultant say?"

"He asked the nonprofit executive if the organization had identified its long-term financing priorities. She said, 'Not yet! But we plan to!' Because of the charity's lack of a long-term finance plan, the donor had to guess at how to designate the best use of his money. If only the organization had partnered with the donor, a mutually beneficial result could have been achieved."

"Mr. Howe, how do you think it makes a donor feel when a charity declines a gift?" I wondered.

He cracked a smile and said, "If the donor is already dead, he probably doesn't mind at all."

I laughed, and he continued: "If the donor is living, obviously he or she should sit down with representatives of the charitable organization and hammer out a mutually agreeable plan. Of course, this can lead to conflict that can become quite contentious. If the charity rejects the donor's restrictions, it may cause great sadness for the donor who, after many years of involvement, may feel he is no longer valued apart from the money he provides."

At this point I felt I was on the cusp of some excellent advice, so I set my iPhone to record and said, "Mr. Howe, I sense that you have some excellent ideas for how to overcome these difficulties." Below is a summary of some things I learned that sunny afternoon.

Mr. Howe's Giving Strategies

1. <u>Challenge Grants</u>: Consider providing a challenge grant. This is an excellent way to engage the organization in a partnership to secure funds. The donor and the organization first need to discuss the purpose and terms of the challenge grant so that it satisfies the needs of the organization while also achieving the philanthropic values of the donor. Such grants provide organizations with leverage to approach other donors to support the project. The challenge grant also gives the organization credibility by showing that someone thought highly enough of their mission to provide such a grant. And the grant has a greater opportunity for success because it involves many people in the project.

2. <u>Best Practices</u>: Require that the recipient operate using best practices before making a gift. This could involve requiring the organization to involve certain numbers and types of governing board leadership. It might also mean developing and adopting appropriate governing policies for managing long-term assets. This may include endowment fund policies, gift acceptance policies that include outright and deferred gifts, investment management policies, endowment

take-out policies, and unrestricted bequest acceptance policies.

3. <u>Accountability</u>: Specify that the organization provide regular reports on its use of the grant money. Achieve quality reporting by creating grant criteria and guidelines that require the faithful application of the best practices as defined by the donor. Reports on the grant can then be made, not only on the charitable use and purpose, but also on the best practice requirements included in the grant guidelines. Sometimes these include reporting on the diversity of the governing board and staff, the establishment of policies and procedures relative to endowment management, and other tangible metrics that best practices attempt to influence.

Look Long-term

Mr. Howe looked doubtfully at my iPhone, so I slid it into my pants pocket as he came nose to nose with me, his beady eyes looking directly into my eyes, making me feel quite uncomfortable as he loudly exclaimed, "We live in a world of instant information, gratification, and experience. Current earnings measure corporate stock prices, and consideration is not always given to long-term financial position and sustainability. Executive decisions of both for-profit and nonprofit corporations are dominated by short-term focus and success. As a result, sometimes short-term decisions negatively impact the organization's ability to develop a long-term sustainable business strategy. This is not good!"

His breath in my face was also not good, so I backed away slightly, but his intensity continued as he said, "You know, donors are in a position to help encourage organizations to orient themselves for long-term success and to adopt a sustainable business model perspective. Adopting a longer view strategic thinking requires that both the governing board and the executive team be in agreement.

"I can tell you that I recently heard of a gift planning professional at a major US educational institution say that they are so focused on the 'here and now' that they would rather receive a $500,000 outright contribution today than a $10 million gift 10 years from now."

I pondered the implications of that mentality as he exclaimed, "How crazy is that! This short-sightedness is amplified by how organizations use gifts received from donor's estates. Generally, they are inclined to spend the entire gift immediately rather than setting aside funds into an endowment to support future financial needs."

Mr. Howe glared at me and almost yelled, "It's that same instant gratification that lands all my homeless friends on the streets!"

Aware that he was over-heating, Mr. Howe took a step backward and pulled out a pair of wire-rimmed glasses. The glasses had round lenses and the wire frame that curled around the ears—the style of glasses that an old time accountant might wear. He played with the glasses while continuing his thoughts:

"I know of a million examples of the pitfalls of instant gratification." He glanced up and down the streets and mentioned a few I won't report here, but soon he came back on task and said, "Take, for example, a situation where a donor established three trusts to pay income to himself and another family member for a 10-year period. After 10 years, the trust distributes its assets to seven charitable organizations. The trust document specifies that the charities must use the funds as an endowment with only four to five percent of the value of the endowment used annually for their charitable purposes."

As Mr. Howe placed the glasses on his face, I said, "That doesn't seem like instant gratification to me. What happened?"

"Well, the Trustee for the trust contacted each of the seven charitable organizations and asked them the following questions:

1. What do you do when you receive gifts from trusts and estates?
2. Do you have an endowment fund? If so, how much do you take out of the fund each year to use for your charitable purpose? Do you use a consistent take-out formula?
3. Do you allow donors to name endowment funds within your overall endowment?
4. Do you have endowment fund policies? What do you do with an endowment fund whose charitable

purpose has become obsolete and needs redirected to another charitable purpose?

5. Have you identified a "menu of endowment opportunities" that donors may use to consider restricting their gifts? Do you allow donors to restrict their gifts?"

"How did the charities respond?" I wondered.

He removed the glasses and used the end of one stem to clean his fingernails and said, "As you might expect, the results were predictable. Four of the seven charitable organizations said they liked to receive estate bequests because it gives them a great jump-start into balancing next year's operating budget.

"This is a one night stand, not a marriage!" he hissed. "Such a response demonstrated a shortsighted view and was not in keeping with the philanthropic goals of the donor or the terms of the trust. As you can imagine, such a mentality did not sit very well with either the trust officer or the donor."

His story squared with my own experience: Most donors do not wish to have their lifetime assets placed into next year's operating budget and immediately spent. Instead, most desire that charities place gifts from their trusts and estates into an endowment fund that will serve as a lasting legacy of them and their support, continuing to assist the organization long after they have passed on.

Recognizing Mr. Howe's passion about the subject, I asked him what donors could do to encourage nonprofit organizations to align their values with the donors' values, visions, and goals.

Placing the wire-rimmed glasses back into his coat pocket, he snapped, "Donors should refuse to be a charitable checking account! Do not automatically send a check to the organization when it sends you the same proposal and request for support that it did the previous year. Be proactive to discover specific projects within the organization that align with your values and philanthropic goals. A contribution of any size can be made using this perspective."

He continued. "When making a donation, always hold the organization accountable. Make sure their mission continues to be relevant and their operations efficient and effective. If the gift is large enough, you can require them to provide annual reports on the specific use of the gift. For smaller contributions, expect to receive some type of feedback on the organization and its work before contributing again."

Mr. Howe placed a very high value on accountability. He said, "When organizations become too complacent, donors can be accomplices in allowing them to exist when they otherwise should go out of business! In other words, a donor's gift may actually do more harm than good."

In my own experience, I have sometimes advised donors to go through a third-party fiduciary agent to receive and facilitate the distribution of a gift that may be beyond the ability of the charity to manage with their existing staff. This helps the charity to care properly for large contributions. Following this process, the donor can create a fund with the fiduciary agent and include all of the required guidelines, criteria, and restrictions of the gift. The third-party fiduciary agent can then hold the organization accountable and require it to meet the guidelines before making the distribution.

I asked Mr. Howe if he had any similar experience. He said, "When I was in the accounting firm, we used to assist our clients by lining up bank trust companies, community foundations, United Way, and other umbrella organizations to serve as fiduciary agents for large contributions."

He seemed distracted now, his mind turning to other matters. I bid him good day and sat down to summarize what I learned. Here is what I wrote: "What Mr. Howe and his glasses focused on today was that by being thoughtful, discerning, and generous, donors can have a significant positive impact on an organization's ability to achieve its mission and purpose. They can also help their beloved charity facilitate its long-term impact on the community well into the future. There is no reason for doing more harm than good."

Chapter 7
Leverage Your Giving

If the gift of one person can be so influential, imagine what a group of donors with the same vision for their gifts could have to significantly impact an organization. —Mr. EH

Promptly at 10:00 a.m. on another Thursday, Mr. Howe showed up at my office, accepted his usual English tea, and sat quietly, his eyes studying his grey suede high-top shoes. I could tell the wheels were turning in his mind under the grey knit cap, and I even wondered if he had spent most of his time in the public library studying about philanthropy since our last meeting.

He looked up at me and asked, "Do you ever wonder what it would be like to be the richest person in the world?"

"I presume everyone wonders that from time to time," I said.

He nodded. "Just think. You would be able to buy anything you want. You would have many 'friends,' but you could never be sure who was truly a friend and who was just trying to get to your money.

"Requests for support would inundate you from charitable organizations all over the world. Everyone would be networking to connect with you to share with you the needs of their organizations. Everywhere you turn, there would be a request for financial support.

"If you were the richest person in the world, when solicited, you would be able to provide for the entire cost of any project you were asked to support. Imagine that an organization in India asks you for a million dollars to build a home for 50 orphans. Your gift would provide all the necessary funding for the entire project. You are passionate about orphan care. Should you agree to give the entire $1 million? Or should you consider leveraging your gift to encourage other donors to be involved in the project as well?"

"I don't know, Mr. Howe," I replied. "I have never thought about that scenario. What do you think?"

"In the short term," he began, "it may seem easier to give the organization the money to construct the home. However, in the long-run, making such a gift may not strengthen the organization's stability to raise ongoing support to take care of those orphans. By not seeking and cultivating new donors, your gift to the organization may actually put it at financial risk over the long-term.

"I once knew a very wealthy man who is a great example of how to leverage gifts effectively," exclaimed Mr. Howe. "His name was Mr. Kenneth Herrick. He owned Tecumseh Products and was president of the Herrick Foundation."

"What did he do that was so effective?" I asked.

"Each year a small college operated a fundraising phone campaign called the Annual Phonathon," replied Mr. Howe. "The Phonathon raised money each year for the operating needs of the college. Volunteers called alumni and friends throughout the country to raise support. Mr. Herrick, through his foundation, granted support to the college each year."

I was perplexed and inquired, "So how did he leverage his annual gift?"

With a sly grin Mr. Howe enthusiastically replied, "Well, rather than simply writing a check to the school, which would've been the easy thing to do, Mr. Herrick instead offered a challenge grant to the college. He would match each dollar contributed by the Phonathon up to $500,000. His gift was significant in that he not only helped the college with his foundation's contribution, but also doubled the amount raised through the Phonathon. His giving technique helped the school identify new donors each year, and his endorsement also gave that educational institution greater credibility. As they say, 'money gets money.'"

He continued with his sly grin, "Over the years, I observed many 'rich folk' take the easy way out and simply write a huge check to a charity. Sure, everyone appreciates the generosity, but by not leveraging a large contribution, a donor may enable an organization to rely too much on a single person's support. When an organization receives a significant percentage of its budget each year from one donor and that donor dies without leaving the organization any type of estate gift [to be discussed in a future chapter], this often results in the organization scrambling for years to come to replenish the lost revenue."

He finally concluded, "Mr. Rockefeller was at one time the richest man in the world, and even he consistently looked for ways to leverage his money to provide maximum support for an organization from a variety of donors. I want to put my money to work the way Mr. Rockefeller did!"

Mr. Howe was passionate about leveraging his charitable gift. He did not want his foundation to simply assist homeless persons; he desired to provide grants that would help homeless persons become self-sufficient, independent, contributing members of society.

"At the library last week I was reading about the Ford Foundation and a number of other foundations that did amazing philanthropic work in leveraging their giving," stated Mr. Howe.

My suspicions were correct! This homeless man must be practically living in the library and making very good use of his time. Now he was viewing a small smooth stone through a magnifying glass he had withdrawn from his bottomless coat pocket.

"S.S. Kresge developed a fantastic formula for leveraging grants," he reported, and then explained how The Kresge Foundation in Troy, Michigan, is one of the long-standing charitable foundations in America. Founded by Sebastian S. Kresge in 1924, for years the foundation made challenge grants to support building programs at churches, schools, and libraries.

The Kresge Foundation had carried out research showing that the first two-thirds of fundraising for the cost of a building project are the easiest to secure. In the beginning of a campaign, many friends and major contributors of a charity will participate. There is typically a lot of enthusiasm and high energy for the project early on. The last one-third of the campaign is the hardest money to secure. As a result, Kresge strategically created a grant formula that provided a challenge grant for the campaign equal to one-third of the final third of the fundraising total.

"The Kresge folks really stretched their grant dollars," admired Mr. Howe, who had turned his magnifying glass to view a blade of grass in his left hand. "For example, if the charity's campaign goal was to raise $3 million to build a new building and they already raised $2 million, The Kresge Foundation grant provided a match of $1 for every $2 raised toward the last $1 million. So, in this example, if the campaign is successful, The Kresge Foundation grant will total $333,334."

In addition to the challenge component, the Kresge strategy also required the organization to use the challenge grant to identify contributions from new sources as well as to motivate current donors to increase their contributions. Typically, the charity would not only achieve its campaign goal, but would also add new and increased donors to their constituency for future support.

Mr. Howe now turned his magnifying glass on me. One eye became very large and he looked a bit like Sherlock Holmes, which was appropriate, for he had sleuthed out the story of one mega-gift that truly made history.

"Robert Winship Woodruff was president of the Coca-Cola Company from 1923 to 1954," Mr. Howe announced. "In 1979, Mr. Woodruff and his brother, George W. Woodruff, gave $105 million to Emory University in Atlanta, Georgia. At the time, it was one of the largest amounts ever given to an institution and not to someone's private foundation. Eventually they would give a total of $230 million to the University."

The Impact of "The Gift"

Almost equally divided between the nineteenth and twentieth centuries, and between its Oxford and Atlanta phases, the history of Emory up until 1979 is largely the story of a respectable regional school that had real substance and a number of distinctive attributes. Their history changed dramatically the day Robert and George Woodruff transferred to Emory the Emily and Ernest Woodruff Fund, comprising $105 million in Coca-Cola stock.

Although Robert had been pouring tens of millions of dollars into Emory for decades, the idea for the transfer of the fund originated with George. Created before the death of their father, Ernest Woodruff, in 1944, the Emily and Ernest Woodruff Foundation had grown with the Coca-Cola Company, whose stock comprised a hundred percent of the foundation's assets.

With a change in tax laws in 1969, the federal government made the income on foundation assets taxable and required foundations to give away five percent of the market value of their assets. Spurred by this, the foundation board—with Robert as chair and George as vice-chair—reorganized the foundation as the Emily and Ernest Woodruff Fund, legally a "supporting organization" exempt from taxation so long as it dedicated its income to specific recipients.

The Woodruff Fund designated Emory to receive 40 percent of its income, and twenty-seven other institutions the remainder. George reportedly kept the checkbook for the fund at his office in the Trust Company Bank building in downtown Atlanta.

Recognizing that others would control the fund after his own death or Robert's, George persuaded his brother that prudence dictated handing over the fund to Emory. George had developed confidence in the ability of Emory's administrators and trustees to manage the assets of the fund, and so, apparently, had Robert.

Over the next year, the Woodruffs and President James Laney negotiated the transfer of the fund. On the day Emory announced the transfer, November 8, 1979, Henry Bowden retired from the board he had chaired for twenty-two years, and Robert Strickland was elected to succeed him. Strickland would remark near the end of his life that he took the job only because Robert Woodruff had insisted that he do so.

"I distinctly remember when the Woodruffs made that gift," recalled Mr. Howe, having deposited the magnifying glass back into his deep left coat pocket. "At the time, it was the largest single gift to any college or university in American history. The gift made a profound impact on Emory University over the next two decades, but the nature of that impact is often misunderstood."

He continued. "While many assume that the infusion of funds would mean few constraints on the budget, the major impact of the gift came from the psychological jolt it had on others. The credibility it gave the university was enormous."

The timing was perfect. In 1979—before "The Gift"—Emory already had the 16th largest endowment among American universities and colleges. A relatively new president had high ambitions for the place and saw the need to raise funds for capital projects and a larger endowment. After a year of studying the feasibility for a campaign, the Executive Committee of the board in July 1979 voted to launch "The Campaign for Emory." Four months later, in November, the full board heard George Woodruff read a letter from his brother announcing the gift of the Woodruff Fund. There were no restrictions on how the money should be used except that the principal should not be encroached upon unless two-thirds of the board determined "that there is an extraordinary need arising out of unforeseen and dire circumstances."

"George and Robert understood the value of endowment for a nonprofit organization," Mr. Howe told me. "They understood the power that such a resource can have in providing stability and impact on a charity."

George Woodruff concluded his remarks by saying, "I hope that each of you here will remember my brother and me in your prayers, that we may have God's protection in our remaining days." The minutes of the meeting record that the board rose for a prolonged ovation.

By the end of the meeting, the trustees went on to approve the campaign, its goal of $160 million made easier by "The Gift." Five years later, under the leadership of Board Chair James B. Williams, The Campaign for Emory concluded with a final tally of $220 million.

Throughout the years, the University has used the Woodruff Fund to create new undergraduate scholarships, graduate fellowships, distinguished professorships, enhancements to academic programs and library collections, and even new buildings. But the most powerful and lasting benefit of the Woodruff gift has been its imperative to look toward the future, to establish long-range goals, and to dream unabashedly about what it would take to make a good university great.

"I have been paying attention to large gifts for many years," noted Mr. Howe. "Since the Woodruff gift to Emory University, there have been many other donations of much greater size. However, what I have observed is a common thread through all of these mega-gifts. It is interesting to me that organizations did not solicit the contributions. Instead, generally donors sought out charities to collaborate in order to achieve their philanthropic objectives."

In these situations, the mega-gift donors were attempting to leverage their philanthropy by collaborating with an existing institution. It is often easier to provide funds to remake an organization rather than starting something from scratch.

"You know, just because you have a lot of money does not automatically guarantee success," exclaimed Mr. Howe. "You need to consider the impact that your mega-gift will have on the charity."

He went on. "For example, if someone contributes a mega-gift to an organization to completely remake and update its services, the personnel within the organization will most likely change as well. These wholesale replacements may turn the culture and character of the organization away from its original identity and make it something other than the institution the donor was attracted to it in the first place."

"That is the beauty of the Emory story," I replied. "The donors worked closely with existing staff and perhaps trained new staff within the same ethos, and thus were able to boost rather than change the trajectory of the institution."

"Precisely," said Mr. Howe. "No matter the size of the gift, the terms and conditions of that gift must be carefully designed to seamlessly mesh with the ethos of the institution. This way the gift will help the organization achieve its mission rather than derail the mission.

"There is power in numbers," he concluded.

I thought he was referring to the number of dollars in a gift, but he was talking about numbers of people. What he said was, "If the gift of one person can be so influential, imagine what a group of donors with the same vision for their gifts could have to significantly impact an organization and its ability to sustain itself and achieve its mission."

Precisely.

Chapter 8
Consider Your Legacy

Understand that pride of accomplishment from one's own hard work is the way to realize true self-esteem, and not from your money. —Mr. EH

"Charity begins at home" is a common phrase, but what is meant by that is not always clear. The speaker might mean "charity is learned at home," or he might be saying, "my children and grandchildren are my charity."

In all of our conversations, Mr. Howe did not mention a wife, children, or grandchildren. He was leaving all of his possessions to his foundation, but in one of our chats—he was chewing on a toothpick stuck in the left side of his mouth—he said, "It is good and important to provide for your family. But how much is enough? Just look around you. In America, even people who are not wealthy have a great many possessions. Given this fact, how much do your children and grandchildren really need?"

I suggested, "especially since the more we have, the more we seem to want."

He cocked an eyebrow and said, "When you consider the amount of money you began your adult life with, it will not take much for you to provide a fantastic jump-start for your children and grandchildren. Helping with college expenses today can be a significant contribution toward leaving a legacy with your family."

I nodded and mentioned that the average cost of a four-year college (public and private) runs at about $135,000. Any adult who helps with those expenses so children or grandchildren do not have student loans is making a significant contribution toward their livelihood.

"Such young folk should be grateful," Mr. Howe stressed. Some students fail to take advantage of that assistance whenever they fail to attend class or go out partying and having a great time. Imagine what those same children would do with a $10,000, $100,000, or $1 million inheritance. Can you honestly trust them with assets that have taken you a lifetime to accumulate?"

"It certainly depends on their character," I suggested. "You would want to approach it on a case-by-case basis."

"Even then it's touchy at best," he countered. "Some apparently level-headed people go berserk with too much cash." Using the tooth pick to poke through the stocking cap and scratch a spot on the back of his scalp, he moved on:

"In addition to the financial support we may want to provide for our children, what other legacy might people with means desire to provide? They may want to consider leaving behind something that will be a lasting testament to their values or beliefs. The manner in which they leave such a legacy will also reflect those values and beliefs."

"What exactly do you have in mind?" I wondered aloud.

He said, "It is right to be concerned that inheriting a lot of money might negatively affect children—or any beneficiary. So my motto here is the same as in the medical profession: Do no harm. I would feel terrible if any inherited wealth would cause or allow any beneficiary of my estate to be less of a person, less accomplished, and of less benefit to themselves, their family, community, and country. Just look at all the people who win the lottery, then immediately quit their jobs, squander their cash, and eventually find themselves worse off than before!"

Mr. Howe snapped the tooth pick in half, poked half of it at me and declared, "more people are harmed by too much money than are hurt by too little money! They receive a financial windfall from an inheritance or a lottery and usually squander it all within 18 months. They may also go into debt beyond their capability to pay, lose their jobs, and experience family break ups, all as a result of too much money."

"That's a serious claim," I acknowledged.

"In fact," he noted, "there is a company in Palm Beach Gardens, Florida, that has a business model to help people going through financial transitions, including lottery winners. The Sudden Money Institute, established in 2000, assists persons going through a financial transition by helping them make wise choices so their lives can be enjoyable and less stressful.

"Instead of concerning yourself with inheriting funds, you should instead appreciate the importance of accomplishing as much as feasible on your own before seeking the help of others," exclaimed Mr. Howe. "In my day, teachers, parents, friends, pastors, librarians, and co-workers were all of great encouragement and support. Life-long learning from all should be a goal you aspire to."

Mr. Howe clearly lived up to this goal himself, even though he lived on the streets. He said, "Instead of living on inherited wealth and doing nothing, you should use the wealth to help enhance your skills, abilities, achievements, and goals. Understand that pride of accomplishment from one's own hard work is the way to realize true self-esteem, and not from your money. In addition to boosting self-esteem, hard work will provide you with a pride of accomplishment, the respect of others, a recognizable reward for work well done, and the discipline that a work schedule provides."

It came to me then that Mr. Howe must be methodical in all his life, which explained why it was always at 10:00 a.m. on Thursday that he turned up to see me. My wandering thoughts came back to attention when he said, "Given the potential negative effect your resources may have on your children, you may wish to consider leaving a legacy through gifting some of *your* funds to set up a charitable foundation or an endowment at your favorite charitable organization."

I do have children and am taking his advice to heart, but what I said to him was this: "Mr. Howe, tell me. How do you go about setting up a charitable foundation or organizational endowment fund?"

"That is what I came to see you about!" He laughed, tucked the two broken pieces of his toothpick back in his pocket, and I took this opportunity to ask him a series of questions designed to help him discern what he should create and how he should create it.

"It's like this," I began. "When someone tells their financial or legal advisors that they want to create a charitable foundation, the first question most often asked by the advisor is 'how much money do you have?'

"That is one of the worst questions that someone can ask," exclaimed Mr. Howe. "Even I know that! I am a great example as to why that question is not relevant at the beginning of the conversation."

I agreed and continued. "A better and more pertinent question to begin with is 'how much involvement do you want personally and for your family in your foundation?' Do you want to conduct charitable activities such as educating children, feeding the homeless, displaying works of art, or assisting with medical needs? Or, would you prefer to grant funds to organizations that conduct those charitable activities?"

"That makes a lot of sense," he observed. "Go on!"

"Another question to ask is, 'do you want to establish this foundation during your lifetime or upon death?' If you do not wish to part with the resources during your lifetime, it is best to establish your charitable foundation vehicle during lifetime that will receive the funding upon your death.

"You also will need to determine who will control and oversee the management functions of the foundation. How much control will your family exercise in selecting charitable grant recipients, both while you are living and when you are gone?"

I continued. "To begin the process of setting up your charitable foundation, you first need to define its purpose. Are you interested in supporting specifically named charities like your church, college or university, or local hospital? Or, do you prefer to have your foundation support various areas of interest such as religion, education, arts and culture? Would you like your foundation to support charitable organizations located in a specific geographic area? Or would you like your foundation to support a blend of all of the above?"

"I did that," interjected Mr. Howe. "I decided I want my foundation to support charitable organizations and activities that assist homeless persons in becoming self-sufficient, independent contributing members of society."

"Yes," I affirmed. "In determining the charitable purpose of your foundation, you also need to understand that your charitable foundation must exercise 'expenditure responsibility.' This means that all grants made are for charitable purposes to qualified public charities. There needs to be proper screening of grant recipients to be sure the Internal Revenue Service recognizes them as qualified public charities."

"Does that mean that I cannot make a grant to my brother and sister-in-law if they routinely take in some of my friends from the street and provide them with temporary shelter and food?" asked Mr. Howe.

"No, Mr. Howe, that would not be allowed," I responded. "But if they created a charitable organization recognized by the IRS to feed and shelter homeless persons and assist them in becoming self-sufficient, independent, contributing members of society, then your foundation could certainly make a grant to support their work."

Continuing, I said, "You will also need to determine if you want your grant-making process to be competitive or non-competitive."

"I never heard of that before. What does that mean?" Mr. Howe inquired.

"It means you decide in advance if you want to receive grant applications from potential grantee organizations or if you wish to pre-select them. You may not realize it, but just because you establish a charitable foundation does not mean that you are required to accept requests for funding. Instead, you may 'pre-select' charitable organizations to which your foundation will make grants."

Mr. Howe seemed quite attentive, so I went on.

"All charitable organizations that you make grants to from your foundation must be public charities established in the United States. You may make grants to organizations outside of United States; however, you need to follow the rules and regulations for international grant making prescribed by the IRS."

"So, what are the different types of charitable foundations that you can establish?" Mr. Howe asked.

"Mr. Rockefeller and I both believe in charitable foundations, but we each have different objectives and may need different types of foundations to achieve our philanthropic goals."

"That's a great question, Mr. Howe," I said. "The first commonly known type of charitable foundation, the kind that Mr. Rockefeller created, is the private foundation. Private foundations are established by individuals, families, or businesses. One advantage of a private foundation is the considerable control that you have over its operation. You can maintain family involvement in grants made both during your lifetime and after your death, and you can control the investment management and administrative functions of the foundation's assets and determine who will govern the foundation for generations to come.

"You can create a private foundation as a nonprofit corporation or a charitable trust. The corporation laws of the state where it is incorporated govern the private foundation established as a nonprofit corporation. The trust laws of the state where it is established govern the private foundation created as a charitable trust.

"The form that you choose may be the most important decision you make in creating your foundation. Over the years, many private foundations have been set up as nonprofit corporations, which cause challenges for individuals who desire to protect and preserve the charitable intent of the foundation as well as sustain their family's involvement."

"What do you mean?" Mr. Howe abruptly asked. "How can setting up a nonprofit corporation cause challenges?"

I thought on how best to answer his question and settled on giving an example: "In the late 1800s, Sebastian S. Kresge founded the Kresge 5 and Dime Company, a discount store, that later became the SS Kresge Company, and in recent years Kmart/Sears. Because of his success, Mr. Kresge wanted to give back to the communities from which he benefited. In 1924, he created The Kresge Foundation. For nearly four decades, the foundation made grants to churches and schools all over the United States. The primary purpose of these grants were for building programs enabling churches and schools to construct facilities to enhance their mission and purpose.

"Mr. Kresge created his foundation as a Michigan nonprofit corporation. A Board of Trustees governs the foundation and is responsible for the care of the foundation assets for the public good.

"The challenge came when Sebastian Spering Kresge passed away in 1966 at the age of 99. The foundation was quite popular at the time and received many applications from churches and schools all over the country. But upon Mr. Kresge's death, members of the foundation's governing Board of Trustees decided they did not want to make grants to churches and schools awarding degrees below the baccalaureate level.

"Grants to churches and schools had become difficult to administer, as they were smaller and required a lot of staff time. The board preferred to spend time making sizeable grants to larger institutions. Rather than making a simple grant-making policy change, the Board of Trustees amended The Kresge Foundation's articles of incorporation and corporate by-laws to prohibit grants to any religious organization, or to organizations controlled by a religious entity, or to schools that offer degrees below the baccalaureate level."

Irritated, Mr. Howe almost shouted, "Do you mean to tell me that a mere corporate board resolution and re-filing papers with the State of Michigan by the foundation's board changed Mr. Kresge's original donor intent?!"

"Yes," I replied. "Because the foundation was created as nonprofit corporation, the trustees were authorized to make such changes. There was no public debate or scrutiny over this decision concerning a charitable foundation with more than $4 billion in assets."

Mr. Howe smacked his right fist into his left palm in an attempt to manage his anger. In a soothing voice I continued to the moral of the story: "Now, Mr. Howe, if The Kresge Foundation were a charitable trust and not a corporation, the Board of Trustees would have been required to receive an order from a court of law to make such a change. That would have made the change of charitable purpose more public and available to public scrutiny. In fact, a judge may not have agreed to such a requested change."

"Are you telling me that if The Kresge Foundation had been in trust form when Mr. Kresge passed away, the board would have had to go to court to restrict grants to churches and schools?"

"That is correct, Mr. Howe."

"Now that is quite interesting," stated Mr. Howe. "Are there any examples where a judge sided with the people requesting such a change?"

"Let me tell you about the Barnes Foundation, in Lower Marion, Pennsylvania," I began. "In the early 1900s, Albert C. Barnes invented a vaccine which earned him millions of dollars.

"Born in 1872 and a graduate of the University of Pennsylvania Medical School, Barnes teamed with a German Chemist named Hermann Hille. Together they developed a mild silver nitrate antiseptic solution which they marketed directly to physicians as the drug Argyrol.

"Argyrol proved effective in treating gonorrhea and proved to prevent gonorrheal blindness in newborn infants. He and Hille formed a company in 1902 and within five years cleared $250,000 in profits (the equivalent of $6.8 million today). Barnes bought out Hille in 1907 and became a millionaire at the age of 35. He eventually sold the business in July 1929 for $6 million.

In addition to his research work as a physician and chemist, Dr. Barnes was an art collector, writer, and educator. His passion, however, was collecting paintings, and he traveled the world collecting some of the world's most prestigious works of art. Today his collection is worth an estimated $20 to $30 billion.

"Creating the Barnes Foundation in 1922, Dr. Barnes formed the foundation as an educational institution, not as a museum. Barnes was critical of the discipline of art history, which he said stifles self-expression and the appreciation of art. So instead of following the traditional museum format, he set up his foundation to allow visitors to have a direct approach to the collection without the interference of curators' thoughts.

"He displayed the artwork in a mansion he had built in Lower Marion, Pennsylvania, designed for that purpose. He required people to write for appointments to see the collection, and he gave preference to students over members of Philadelphia society. Applicants sometimes received rejection letters 'signed' by Barnes' dog, Fidele-de-Port-Manech. He refused admission to writer James A. Michener who later gained access to the collection by posing as an illiterate steelworker. In another case, Barnes turned down the poet T.S. Eliot's request with the one word response, 'Nuts.'"

Mr. Howe applauded and exclaimed, "I think I would have liked this Mr. Barnes!"

"No doubt about that," I agreed, then continued. "Mr. Barnes was very concerned about major Philadelphia art institutions taking over his collection. He watched how the Philadelphia Museum of Art took control of the collection of his late attorney, John Johnson, and he tried to prevent the same thing from happening to his collection.

"One technique he used to protect his collection was to place it into a charitable trust. The trust agreement required that the foundation remain an educational institution open to the public only on selective days. It also required that the collection could not be loaned or sold and was to remain on the walls in the mansion in exactly the places the works were located at the time of his death.

"In addition, upon his death due to a traffic collision in 1951, Barnes contributed $1 million to the trust to serve as an endowment fund to support the operation of the foundation."

Mr. Howe winked and said, "Barnes must have known that in order to change the terms of a trust agreement you need to receive the approval of a judge."

"I believe that is true," I replied. "Why else would he have gone to such great lengths to provide all of the restrictive language in the trust agreement?

"The upshot is that in order to carry out Dr. Barnes' desire to keep the foundation as an educational institution and not a museum, the trustees allowed art students to view the works of art four days each week. The fifth day they allowed for public viewing, which created huge traffic problems. Busloads of people came each week to the residential neighborhood where his mansion was located to see the fantastic art. This heavy traffic became a burden to the neighborhood.

"Mr. Barnes should have thought ahead and torn down the house next door for parking space," Mr. Howe blurted.

I continued. "Albert Barnes' father, a butcher by trade, lost his right arm at the Battle of Cold Harbor during the American Civil War. After the war, he worked as a letter carrier. His mother was a devout Methodist who regularly took young Albert to African-American camp meetings and revivals.

"In the late 1940s, Barnes met Horace Mann Bond, the first black president of Lincoln University, a historically black college located in Chester County, Pennsylvania. Their friendship led to Barnes inviting Lincoln students to view the collection and insured President Bond that the University would have a prominent role in the foundation after his death. The result is that Barnes ultimately gave the authority to the Board of Trustees of Lincoln University to appoint the foundation's board of trustees each year."

Mr. Howe applauded, clapping both of his hands vociferously. "Bravo to Dr. Barnes for his commitment to diversity and equality in America—a man ahead of his time."

"But possibly not far enough ahead," I continued. "You see, the $1 million endowment eventually dwindled to nothing. The trustees were looking for ways to increase revenue, and after a lengthy court battle in 1992, the Barnes Foundation Trustees received permission from the court to send 80 of the art works on a tour to generate funds. The tour attracted huge crowds in all of the cities where it appeared, raising more than $16 million for the foundation's operations."

"Wow, that must be some art!" interjected Mr. Howe.

"Yes," I replied. "However, even with the influx of new operating capital, the trustees needed to develop a more sustainable financial plan for the foundation. And that was when the City of Philadelphia and three large regional charitable private foundations approached them to consider moving into the city and allow greater public access to the collection.

"The three foundations committed a total of $150 million to move the foundation to the city: $100 million to build a facility in the art district in downtown Philadelphia, and another $50 million to serve as an endowment to fund ongoing operations."

"Some good ideas there," said Mr. Howe, "but they violate the terms of Mr. Barnes' conditions in his charitable trust. He would have rejected those uppity socialites in favor of the starving artists. So, did it go to court?"

"It certainly did," I replied. "In an effort to provide for a sustainable financial model for the foundation's future, the Trustees of the Barnes Foundation petitioned the court to move the collection to Philadelphia. The hearings took many months and numerous articles appeared in the *Wall Street Journal,* the *Chronicle of Philanthropy,* and a book and documentary film were produced titled *The Art of the Steal.*

"But in the end," I said, "and as you probably suspect, the judge ruled to allow the trust to be changed and the artwork moved from Lower Marion to its new home in Philadelphia which opened in May 2012."

"What could have persuaded the judge to go against the wishes of Mr. Barnes?" Mr. Howe wondered.

"The task of an impartial judge," I suggested "is to not only look at Dr. Barnes' charitable intent, but also to look into the best interest of the public. The public interest is reflected in the fact that it is the federal government that affords us charitable tax benefits for our contributions to our private foundations. This gives the public some vested interest in private foundations, and thus the judge held the foundation to a higher standard to help meet the public good."

"I would like to investigate this notion of public interest in private wealth at greater length," said Mr. Howe, "but not today—and I may not be back next week." As he talked, he reached more deeply into his pockets than I had seen him go before—under the coat and into his pants pocket—and he came up with a heavily battered, brown wallet. He extracted a $100 bill, shook it in his fist and said, "Do you know what I will do with this?"

"I cannot imagine!"

"I am off to the bus station. I am going to Philadelphia to have a look at Mr. Barnes' art museum."

Chapter 9
Public Interest in Private Funds

I thought that if you set up a charitable foundation, it is private. —Mr. EH

I missed Mr. Howe the following Thursday morning, but I spent some of my time frequently devoted to him by looking at the Barnes Foundation website at http://www.barnesfoundation.org/ to enjoy a vicarious tour of billions of dollars' worth of great art, and to discover that Dr. Barnes' old art mansion in Merion is now at the heart of a 12-acre arboretum established by his wife, Laura, specifically to serve as an outdoor classroom.

This astonishing collection has 3,000 unusual species of woody plants, 31 state champion trees, and other collections of flowers, medicinal plants, and hardy ferns. I went on my coffee break full of gratitude for the public benefit afforded to me by the private wealth and wise stewardship of Dr. Albert and Laura Barnes.

"I thought that if you set up a charitable foundation, it is private," Mr. Howe said when I saw him the next week. "How can the government and the public in general learn about how my private foundation is operating?"

"Great question, Mr. Howe," I responded. "Private foundations provide you with considerable control, but they are subject to stringent rules, regulations, and taxes. In fact, private foundations are not private after all. The Internal Revenue Service considers the tax return of a private foundation to be of public record. As a result, all private foundation tax returns are available to the public either on the internet or by requesting a copy from the foundation (which the foundation has to provide to you within 30 days of your request). The private foundation tax return includes all of the detailed information of the foundation including any paid salaries to staff and a listing of all of the investment holdings and grants made."

Mr. Howe interjected, "That's not private. They should not call it a private foundation if it is so public!"

"The private foundation must also pay a tax on its net investment earnings," I informed him. "Although the tax rate is small (1% - 2%), it still is an expense to the foundation. In addition, the private foundation has to make a minimum distribution amount each year to charitable organizations."

"Oh, really?" Mr. Howe inquired. "How do you figure out the required amount?"

"You calculate the minimum distribution amount by taking the average monthly value of the foundation over the 12 months of the year and multiplying by 5%. For example, if the average balance of the foundation for the past 12 months equaled $100,000, then the foundation must grant the minimum distribution amount of $5,000 (5%) to charities. If charities do not receive this amount over a three-year period, then the entire amount is paid to the government in the form of an excise tax."

"I did not know that," said Mr. Howe. "I always thought that charitable foundations did not pay taxes."

I continued. "Another challenge in creating a private foundation in corporate form is that it creates the potential for outsiders to 'highjack' the foundation away from the family of the founder. Although creating a nonprofit corporation provides great flexibility, sometimes current board members appoint their friends to the board instead of family members. This could not be truer than what happened at the Ford Foundation."

"Exactly!" Mr. Howe exclaimed. "I saw that happen first-hand in my work with Mr. Ford and the foundation."

"Let me tell you what I understand happened, and see if you can fill in some of the details, Mr. Howe," I said.

"Henry Ford and his son, Edsel, established the Ford Foundation with an initial gift of $25,000 on January 15, 1936. Created as a Michigan nonprofit corporation under the leadership of Ford family members, the charitable purposes of the foundation were broad in scope, making grants to many kinds of charities.

"In the early years of the foundation, members of the Ford family made grants from the foundation to support Detroit area organizations that Henry Ford had helped to establish such as Henry Ford Hospital, Greenfield Village, and Henry Ford Museum.

"After the deaths of Edsel Ford in 1943 and Henry Ford in 1947, it became clear that the Ford Motor Company stock they left to the foundation in their estates would create the largest philanthropic entity in the world. So the foundation's board of trustees, led by Henry Ford II, Edsel's son, commissioned a study to chart the institution's future.

"The seven-member Gaither Study Committee, headed by future Ford Foundation president H. Rowan Gaither, a respected San Francisco lawyer, recommended that the foundation become a national and international philanthropy dedicated to the advancement of human welfare. Perhaps most significantly, the panel urged the foundation to focus on solving humankind's most pressing problems, whatever they might be, rather than work in any particular field."

Mr. Howe reflected, "It is obvious that the young Mr. Ford realized the foundation would have considerably more money to give away each year beyond the foundation's traditional grant-making to the Michigan charities his grandfather helped to establish. The Gaither Study guided his attempt to provide proper stewardship over a very large fund."

"I think you are onto something, Mr. Howe," I replied. "Here are some of the recommendations of the study." I knew he would be asking me about these matters and had prepared a slip of paper for him with the following information, a summary of the policies embraced by the Ford Foundation in 1949 and published in 1950:

Promise significant contributions to world peace and the establishment of a world order of law and justice

Secure greater allegiance to the basic principles of freedom and democracy in the solution of the insistent problems of an ever-changing society

Advance the economic well-being of people everywhere and improve economic institutions for the better realization of democratic goals

Strengthen, expand, and improve educational facilities and methods to enable individuals to realize more fully their intellectual, civic, and spiritual potential; to promote greater equality of educational opportunity; and to conserve and increase knowledge and enrich our culture

Increase knowledge of factors that influence or determine human conduct, and extend such knowledge for the maximum benefit of individuals and society

Mr. Howe commented, "Some of those recommendations align with my foundation's goals."

"So far, so good," I said. "The report also recommended that the foundation operate under the general guidance of the trustees, with the president and staff officers having a high degree of discretion and flexibility to respond to unforeseen issues and new opportunities.

"Under the direction of Henry Ford II, the trustees took a further step to fulfill the foundation's new national and global mission by deciding to move the foundation offices from Dearborn, Michigan, to New York, New York."

"That's right," Mr. Howe jumped in. "That was in 1953 and the first time I met Mr. Rockefeller at Tavern on the Green."

"You remember correctly," I said. "And as you know, Henry Ford II was a key figure in the foundation from 1943 to 1976. Serving those years as president, chair, and member of the board of trustees, he oversaw its transformation from a local Detroit-area foundation to a national and international organization. The goal in most of his major decisions was to create an institution of the highest order to pursue innovative solutions to the problems of humankind.

"Under the leadership of Henry Ford II, the foundation sought to divest itself of Ford Motor Company stock (which went public in 1955). Discussions began as early as 1949 on the diversification of the foundation's portfolio. Divestment of the Ford Motor Company stock took place between 1955 and 1974."

Mr. Howe interjected, "I think Mr. Ford wanted to separate the family business from the foundation."

"That very well could be, Mr. Howe," I replied. "At any rate, the foundation also expanded its governing and staff leadership to include individuals beyond members of the Ford family until a majority were not Ford family members. As early as 1950 the foundation trustees appointed Paul G. Hoffman as president to succeed Henry Ford II. Hoffman was influential in moving the foundation from Michigan to New York.

"Implementing the Gaither Study and moving to New York facilitated the gradual shift to more and more grants made to other parts of the country and world. Today the residents of the Detroit area and the state of Michigan receive very little benefit from the wealth generated by one of their most famous and influential citizens. Finally, in 1976, Henry Ford II, the last member of the Ford family to be part of the governing board of the foundation, resigned his position as a trustee."

"Mr. Ford could have changed the world from Detroit just as easily as from New York." Mr. Howe observed. "It was almost like a king abdicating his throne!"

"There may be something to that," I replied. "If the Ford Foundation had been created as a charitable trust, the language could have required that a certain number—even a majority—of the board of trustees be lineal descendants of the Ford family. Such a provision might have headed off the subtle coup that took place over many years in the governance of the foundation.

"Today, the Ford Foundation remains committed to advancing human welfare. Headquartered in New York City, it makes grants in all 50 states and, through 10 regional offices around the world, supporting programs in more than 50 countries. Trustees have come from the United States, Latin

America, Africa, and Asia and have brought experience in business, government, higher education, law, nonprofit management, and the civic sector with a diversity of approaches and continuity of purpose."

"I guess Mr. Ford's wishes are coming true," said Mr. Howe. "But do you think the trust form is that much better than the corporate form in protecting and preserving family involvement and charitable intent when setting up a charitable foundation?"

"I think so," I replied. "It depends on your personal preferences and situation. But most people want to keep family members involved in the foundation throughout the generations of their families, as well as maintaining the charitable purposes that reflect their values, vision, and goals."

I went on. "Many think that because a foundation has a lot of money, it needs to be established as a nonprofit corporation similar to the Ford Foundation. However, another great example of a large foundation that was formed as a charitable trust is the W.K. Kellogg Foundation."

"I love Corn Flakes," said Mr. Howe. He pointed west and murmured, "They come from just over there in Battle Creek, Michigan."

I continued. Then you probably know that in 1930, breakfast cereal pioneer Will Keith Kellogg created The W.K. Kellogg Foundation as a Michigan charitable trust. Mr. Kellogg defined its purpose as, 'administering funds for the promotion of the welfare, comfort, health, education, feeding, clothing, sheltering and safeguarding of children and youth, directly or indirectly, without regard to sex, race, creed, or nationality.' To guide current and future trustees and staff, he said to use the money as you please so long as it promotes the health, happiness, and well-being of children.

"Mr. Kellogg had a pretty simple philanthropic vision," stated Mr. Howe. "And you know, he had a passion to help children. However, I prefer to eat the Sugar Frosted Flakes, myself. I really like that Tony the Tiger."

"I like the Sugar Frosted Flakes as well," I agreed. "And I like the success of the W.K. Kellogg Child Welfare Foundation. And the language in the trust requires that the primary offices always reside in Battle Creek, Michigan. Because the foundation is in trust form, any change to these provisions needs approval from a court of law. Although the foundation now has $7.5 billion in assets and is one of the largest charitable foundations in the world, it continues to operate under the terms of the agreement as drafted in 1930."

Mr. Howe said, "That Mr. Kellogg had a simple vision and a simple setup. He knew what he wanted to do with his money to have a lasting positive impact on our world. He kept things simple and did not attempt to control the future with highly restrictive language in the trust agreement. That appears to have made a difference making his foundation a significant player in our society over the past five generations."

Mr. Howe then said, "Maybe I'm asking you to help me to set up my foundation more like Mr.

Kellogg than like Mr. Rockefeller! But in either case, what things do I need to think about as we move forward?"

"You need to consider five primary management areas for your foundation," I replied.

"First, to account for the assets, you need to place them under the care and custody of a reputable financial institution.

"Second, you need to invest the assets properly, meeting all of the prudent investor rules and regulations for investments of a charitable foundation. You can have the custody and investment management of the assets handled by the same institution. Or, you can choose separate institutions for each service. You may want to place the assets with a proper fiduciary to insure they are not subject to potential embezzlement.

"Third, you will want to work with your asset advisors to create an investment policy statement that will define the objectives of the investments of the funds. The investment policy statement should identify an asset allocation for the investments that will be consistent with the short- and long-term goals of the foundation and its annual distribution requirements.

"Fourth, you will need to file all of the necessary paperwork with the federal and state governments to make sure your foundation follows the law. You will want to involve professionals who understand the laws relative to federal and state compliance and excise taxes. These professionals will keep you out of trouble and make sure that all required government taxes are paid and reports filed.

"You will also need to make sure your foundation operates properly relative to both the law as well as best practices. We achieve this by putting in place governance and organizational operating structures for your foundation.

"You can also seek professional assistance concerning the organizational management of the foundation. Its requirements will vary depending on the type of vehicle that you use for your foundation. For example, if your foundation is set up as a nonprofit corporation, you will need to convene the governing board by sending meeting notices according to the requirements of the by-laws of the corporation. As long as you comply with the law, you may establish any kind of management structure you wish to use, whether the foundation is a nonprofit corporation or a charitable trust.

"Finally, you will have to make sure your foundation makes grants to qualified public charities for the charitable purposes that you seek to support. We accomplish this by creating grant guidelines and a formal application that charitable organizations can use when applying for grants."

"That's a lot of information to remember," said Mr. Howe. "It appears that Mr. Spears was wise in sending me to you to set up my foundation like Mr. Rockefeller—or maybe like Mr. Kellogg. There is a lot to know about this foundation business."

"You are right, as usual, Mr. Howe," I replied. "There certainly is."

Chapter 10
Where the Rubber Hits the Road

Actually giving away the money is when a person's philanthropic goals are realized. —Mr. EH

The next time Eugene Howe came to visit, it was quickly evident that his mental wheels were still turning. He had moved beyond the complexities of establishing a foundation to the practical questions of how the foundation would make grants. What he said was, "I know that the grant-making activity is where the rubber hits the road for a charitable foundation. Actually giving away the money is when a person's philanthropic goals are realized."

"Well said," I agreed. "In getting started on the grant making for your foundation, you will first want to set the parameters by establishing grant-making guidelines. These guidelines are essential no matter whether your foundation makes grants to pre-determined organizations or through a more competitive application process.

"You will have to decide the following:

- Settle on the size and number of grants you wish to make annually.
- Determine whether you will make multi-year grant commitments or distribute grants on a year-to-year basis.

- Figure out if you would rather pre-select the recipients or use a 'competitive application process.' Either way, your foundation will need to formulate grant guidelines."

"What do you mean by a 'competitive application process'?" he asked.

"That's where you establish a grant-making process including an application form, submission deadlines, grant-making priorities and restrictions, a system for proposal review, a timeline, and grant evaluation requirements.

"There are nearly as many grant-making policies and procedures as there are foundations. However, you may be able to find a sample common grant application form if you look online. Do you have a computer, Mr. Howe," I inquired.

"No," he replied. "But I am learning to use one at the library. Tell me. Why can't I just make grants when I want to make them? Why do I need all these guidelines?"

"Well, if you want charitable organizations to apply for a grant from your foundation, they will need to know when they can apply and what information you expect from them," I answered. "However, if you do not want to deal with all of the formality, then you can go with the non-competitive approach."

"How would that work?" he asked.

"In the non-competitive format, the foundation makes grants only to selected organizations as long as they continue to meet certain criteria. The criterion include maintaining their qualified public charity status, and maintaining the specific charitable purposes that you intend for the grant funds. Those who govern your foundation need to be sure that they achieve your philanthropic intent through the organization's stated charitable purposes."

"What if those who govern my foundation prove irresponsible?" Mr. Howe wanted to know.

I said, "That happens. I know of a number of examples where the foundation administrator did not fulfill this responsibility, and a court of law removed the funds from the control of that administration. For example, back on May 30, 1975, Mrs. Beryl H. Buck died and left a will establishing the Buck Trust. Her will said the Buck Trust 'shall always be held and used for exclusively nonprofit charitable, religious or educational purposes in providing care for the needy in Marin County, California, and for other nonprofit charitable, religious or educational purposes in that county.'

"In 1979, the court appointed the San Francisco Foundation as distribution trustee of the Buck Trust and named Wells Fargo Bank and Mrs. Buck's personal lawyer and friend John Elliott Cook as investment co-trustees.

"Mrs. Buck's estate closed in 1980 when the probate court funded the Buck Trust with approximately $260 million. At that time, the probate court specifically reserved oversight over the Buck Trust and required ongoing accountability reports from the San Francisco Foundation.

"About four years after its appointment as distribution trustee, the San Francisco Foundation filed a modification petition in the Marin County probate court seeking permission to modify the trust agreement and allow them to spend a portion of the Buck Trust income outside the borders of Marin County. In essence, the petition asked the court to apply the *cy pres* doctrine that essentially changes the charitable purpose of the trust to a purpose that is close to the original.

"The rationale given for the requested change was because the size of the Buck Trust income and the relative affluence of Marin County residents made it 'inexpedient to continue to expend all of the income from the Buck Trust solely within Marin County.'"

"That administrator had no imagination!" Mr. Howe exclaimed. "Why couldn't they go out and discover the needs in the county, locate organizations to address them, and make grants to support the needs they identified?"

"Now you are thinking like Mrs. Buck's personal attorney and the representatives of Marin County," I affirmed. "In response to the petition for modification, John Elliott Cook, Marin County, and the Marin Council of Agencies filed a petition to remove the San Francisco Foundation as distribution trustee.

"In addition, the probate court permitted numerous parties to intervene in the action. Ultimately, two of the parties to the litigation — the San Francisco Foundation and a group of 46 charities — sought to modify the trust by removing the Marin-only restriction, while five — the Attorney General, Marin County, Marin Council of Agencies, John Elliott

Cook, and Wells Fargo Bank — opposed the petition for modification."

"It sounds like there was a geographic feud for the money," Mr. Howe observed.

"That's my impression, too. After a six-month trial, the probate court issued a 136-page decision refusing to apply the *cy pres* doctrine to modify the Marin-only charitable purpose restriction in the trust. The court reasoned that all of the Buck Trust income can be distributed effectively and efficiently in Marin County. Moreover, the court found that the geographic restriction in the Buck Trust was 'unequivocal.'"

"So the judge agreed with me!" Mr. Howe exclaimed. "He determined there is no question that the geographic restriction of the trust agreement could be fulfilled."

"Yes," I said. "Plus, the probate court found that Mrs. Buck intended that the benefits of grants made in Marin County 'would and should extend beyond Marin's borders.' According to the interpretation of the court, Buck Trust funds could benefit projects and purposes beyond Marin County so long as the funds themselves were spent in Marin County. Such projects might include a social policy institute, an environmental research center, or a center on aging."

"Well done!" Mr. Howe said. "That means Marin County could carry out charitable activities that reached all the way into San Francisco—and beyond."

"That's correct, Mr. Howe," I replied. "And there is more to the story. Before and during trial to modify the trust, the parties engaged in negotiations concerning the removal of the distribution trustee. The Honorable Homer B. Thompson, a Santa Clara County trial judge assigned by the State Supreme Court to preside over the Buck Trust litigation, orchestrated these negotiations.

"Late in the trial the San Francisco Foundation surprised the court by offering to resign as distribution trustee, provided it could recover its attorney fees."

"Success!" exclaimed Mr. Howe. "I propose a toast to The Honorable Judge Thompson!" and he plucked a small silver metal flask from his pocket, held it high, and offered it to me. I paused a moment, a bit stunned. All along, I wondered if Mr. Howe had a drinking problem and whether that was what resulted in his homeless status. The look on my face must have been one of bashfulness and awkwardness all in one.

"What's the matter?" he asked. "You look like you have seen a ghost!"

"Oh, thank you, Mr. Howe," I managed to reply. "Thank you for your kind offer. I would rather not have anything to drink right now."

"Too bad," he said. "This apple juice from McDonald's is really good. I keep it in this flask I found to prevent spilling apple juice all inside my coat pockets." So saying, he tipped back his head, said "To The Honorable Judge Thompson!" and took a swig of juice. Wiping his lips, he said, "Now then, tell me about the rest of that settlement surrounding the resignation of the San Francisco Foundation."

"Oh yes," I said. "There were actually two settlements. In the first settlement, the San Francisco Foundation agreed to resign as distribution trustee, and Marin County and the Marin Council of Agencies agreed to petition the probate court to appoint a new entity—the Marin Community Foundation—as successor trustee.

"The second settlement established a procedure for selecting the governing board of the successor trustee—the Marin Community Foundation—and for monitoring its administration of trust. The parties petitioned the court for an order requiring the successor trustee to designate a significant portion of the Buck Trust income to fund 'major projects' in Marin County that will be of national and international importance and will benefit all humankind."

"When did this happen?" Mr. Howe wondered.

I said, "The order appointing the successor trustee was filed on July 31, 1986, and provides that the new trustee distribute at least 20% of the annual gross income of the Buck Trust to projects which will 'inure to Marin County residents and to all of humankind.' To the extent practical, the projects are to address subjects in which Beryl Buck had an interest during her lifetime and consistent with her desire to bring respect and admiration to Marin County."

"Ah," said Mr. Howe, rubbing his hands together. "So, what projects did they fund?"

"The first three were the Buck Center for Research in Aging, the Marin Institute for the

Prevention of Alcohol and Other Drug Problems, and the Beryl Buck Institute for Education. The three projects received a total of $27.3 million in Buck Trust funding. All three projects are now established and operating as charitable organizations that rely heavily on Buck Trust funding."

"And how much funding might that be?" Mr. Howe wanted to know.

"Today, the Buck Trust has approximately $750 million in assets and has granted nearly $800 million in continuing support of the three projects as well as other charitable organizations throughout Marin County.

"But my reason for telling you this story is to stress that your foundation managers need to be faithful and true to your philanthropic goals long after you are gone."

"They sure had better be!" he agreed. "What you help me establish will be their guidepost."

Chapter 11
DAF and CLT Alternatives

Smart as he was, Mr. Rockefeller made sure he had
professionals assisting him with his foundation, too.
—Mr. EH

"Okay," Mr. Howe began. He sat in his usual spot, sipping his usual English tea. "I think I understand the difference between competitive and non-competitive grant making, and foundations in trust form versus corporation form. But your examples all involve millions and millions of dollars. Is there a more simple way to set up and make grants for the little guy?"

"Yes, there absolutely is," I exclaimed. "Not only is it simple and easy, it doesn't cost anything to establish. The problem is that you don't have as much control as you do with a private foundation."

"What do you call this?" Mr. Howe asked as he crossed his legs and sipped his tea.

"It's called the Donor Advisor Fund (DAF) and it has gained popularity since the early 1990s. It received its legal definition by Congress through the enactment of the Pension Protection Act of 2006. In fact, Mr. Howe, this is the vehicle I am using to create your charitable foundation."

"Do you mean to say you are setting up my foundation, like Mr. Rockefeller, in the form of a donor advisor fund?"

"Absolutely. Although Mr. Rockefeller's foundation is a private foundation and your foundation is a Donor Advisor Fund, from a philanthropic perspective they function the same."

The Donor Advisor Fund

He didn't say anything, just pursed his lips and waited.

"Let me further explain," I said. "A Donor Advisor Fund is not a legal entity. Instead, it is a part of another charitable entity. Usually the umbrella charitable organization is a community foundation or other public charity with broad charitable purposes. Some colleges, universities, and hospitals offer Donor Advisor Fund programs. The grants that are made from those programs are often restricted to the charitable purposes of the umbrella organization. For example, if a college offers a Donor Advisor Fund program, any grants from the donor advised fund may be restricted to educational institutions and programs."

Continuing, I said, "In setting up a Donor Advisor Fund, you enter into a donor contribution agreement with the parent organization. This agreement defines the charitable purpose of the fund and identifies the current and future fund advisors. These advisors are able to recommend grants made from the fund to specific charities. The parent organization then accepts or rejects the grant recommendations received from the advisors."

You could see the wheels turning in Mr. Howe's mind. "Are you saying that if I put money into my foundation while I am alive, I can send you a request to make a grant, and you will send the organization the money?"

"Most of the time, Mr. Howe, as long as the grant recommendation is consistent with the charitable purposes of the parent organization in their guidelines for the donor advisor fund program and the charitable purposes in the donor contribution agreement."

I added, "In contrast, if you establish a private foundation instead, as long as the grants are made according to the requirements of the law and the charitable purposes of the foundation, you do not need to recommend or request grants, you simply make them.

"Compared to the private foundation, the Donor Advisor Fund is a simpler way to establish your charitable foundation," I told him.

"You may not have as much control as you would creating a private foundation. However, you and your family may be able to spend more time involved with the charitable organizations and their activities and experience the joy of supporting those activities rather than having to take the time to address the management responsibility for your foundation.

"By working with another charitable organization, you rely on them to administer everything properly. The IRS has instituted significant penalties and taxes on individuals who mismanage their charitable foundations. Establishing a Donor Advisor Fund may insulate you from any such potential penalties and taxes."

"Gad zooks," he said. "I do not mess with the IRS! Am I ever glad Mr. Spears sent me to see you to establish my foundation like Mr. Rockefeller."

"Even the individuals and families that create private foundations often set up a corresponding donor advised fund," I mentioned. "That way they can control all the assets of the foundation and the family involvement through the private foundation. The foundation simply makes one grant annually of its minimum distribution amount to its Donor Advisor Fund. The foundation then recommends grants from its Donor Advisor Fund to selected charities, thereby ensuring proper compliance with government regulations as well as receiving technical assistance and support from the parent charity that operates the DAF program."

"Very nice," Mr. Howe commented, and his comment reminded me of an important additional fact.

"It also enables the foundation to make grants to organizations anonymously, as it can make a DAF grant under the name of the parent organization and not the name of the donor fund. So you can see why DAFs have become a good way to create a charitable foundation."

The Charitable Lead Trust

Mr. Howe seemed pleased to understand why I was setting up his foundation as a Donor Advisor Fund, but he was a relentless seeker of more information and he said, "Is that my only option?"

I replied, "There is one other less common, yet highly effective trust that can be used as a charitable foundation. It is called a Charitable Lead Trust. Here is how it works. You create a Charitable Lead Trust in a similar fashion to a private foundation. This trust arrangement allows you to transfer assets into the trust over a period of years. You can make the trust for as short or as long as you would like, including throughout the rest of your life.

"Each year, the trustee distributes an amount of funds to charitable organizations that you specify, either in the trust document or to organizations that you personally select. At the end of the term of the trust, the trustee distributes all of the assets back to you or to your family depending upon the type of Charitable Lead Trust you create. Like the private foundation, this is a taxable trust, but the tax rate is considerably higher."

"Wow," exclaimed Mr. Howe, who had been removing his left shoe as I was speaking, and now he was removing his sock. "You mean to tell me that you can put money into a trust and then get it back?"

"That's right, Mr. Howe," I said. "You can have the trust assets sent back to you or you can have them go to your family. It's a nice arrangement for someone who doesn't currently need the income from the assets but at some point in the future will want to get the money back for themselves, or to give to their family."

Mr. Howe scratched the arch of his foot and I issued to him my usual caution: "Mr. Howe, you need to know there are plenty of pitfalls that can arise in operating all of the types of vehicles we have talked about that you can use to create your charitable foundation."

"Such as...?"

"They include potential acts of self-dealing, inappropriate grant payments or investments, or improper management of the foundation. These issues may lead to significant personal taxes and penalties."

"That explains everything," Mr. Howe said as he cleaned between the toes on his left foot with the index finger on his right hand. "Smart as he was, Mr. Rockefeller made sure he had professionals assisting him with his foundation, too!"

Tax Considerations

I told Mr. Howe that leaving money from an estate to any form of charitable foundation receives equal tax benefits to the estate. However, there are significant differences when contributing to the same charitable foundations during your lifetime. These differences depend on the size of charitable contribution deductions you can claim from your taxable income.

"You did tell me that you have a current tax problem," I reminded Mr. Howe. "Maybe you will want to place some money in your foundation now to help offset your income tax liability. I am not pushing you to do so, it's simply an option to consider." I went on to describe the tax deduction differences in giving to various types of foundations during a person's lifetime.

"The first difference concerns the maximum amount you are able to deduct in any given tax year. If you give cash to a private foundation, you may deduct the full amount of your contribution up to 30% of your adjusted gross income. If you give more than 30 %, you are allowed to carry forward any unused deduction up to five additional years."

You could see the math wheels turning in Mr. Howe's accountant head. He inquired, "If I gave $5,000 to a private foundation and my income was $10,000, I can only deduct $3,000 of the contribution from my tax return. I can then deduct the remaining $2,000 portion of the gift next year assuming that I have income. Is that correct?"

"Yes, Mr. Howe. You have that correct," I replied. "On the other hand, if you contribute cash to a Donor Advisor Fund, you would be able to deduct up to 50% of your adjusted gross income with the five-year carry forward provision. For smaller contributions, this difference is not material. However, when making large contributions, this difference in the deduction limits can be significant," I noted.

"Another thing: If you contribute publicly traded securities instead of cash, you may deduct the full fair market value subject to the limitation of 20% of adjusted gross income for a gift to a private foundation and 30% for gift to a donor advised fund."

It was clear he understood all of that, so I added, "Probably the most significant difference in deductions allowed for gifts to charitable foundations is in gifting 'hard-to-value' assets. These assets include real estate, closely held business interests, partnerships, and collectible items.

"For example if you have real estate that you would like to contribute to your private foundation, you may only deduct the lesser of the fair market value or your cost basis. However, you may contribute the same piece of real estate to create your Donor Advisor Fund and deduct the full fair market value of the contribution, subject to the same limitations as I previously stated."

"Give me an example," Mr. Howe commanded.

"Ok," I replied. "Let's say you have some property—not your personal residence—currently appraised at $500,000 and you bought the property for $200,000. If you deed that property over to a private foundation, your charitable contribution deduction will be equal to the $200,000 cost basis. If instead, you gift the property to a Donor Advisor Fund, then your charitable contribution deduction will be the full fair market value of $500,000. This difference can provide significant tax savings depending on your personal income circumstances."

"Good," said Mr. Howe. He had his sock back on and was working at lacing up his boot. "There's another reason I'm glad to be creating a Donor Advisor Fund."

I continued. "Another hard-to-value asset is closely held stock. If you are a business owner looking to avoid paying capital gains tax on the sale of your business, gifting a portion of your closely held stock to a Donor Advisor Fund in advance of the sale of the business could yield a significant tax deduction, avoid the capital gains tax, and preserve money to achieve your philanthropic goals.

"Often business owners have a zero cost basis in their closely held stock as they established their businesses with virtually nothing. If during their lifetime they contributed some of this appreciated stock to establish a private foundation, the charitable contribution deduction they may claim will be zero. Gifting the same stock to establish a Donor Advisor Fund allows them to deduct the full market value of that stock and avoid paying capital gains tax on its appreciation."

"See here," said Mr. Howe. "This is valuable information. I think you should write a book."

Chapter 12
21st Century Philanthropy

This extraordinary amount of money demands and deserves careful planning and education. We care not just about the transfer of our property, but also the transfer of our personal values. —Mr. EH

Mr. Howe believed that being an example for the next generation was one of the most important legacies a person could give. He told me, "Although it is a natural instinct to want to help your fellow man, it is a learned behavior to share what you have with others. The simplest example is teaching little children to share their toys. Three toddlers in a room with three different toys will all want to play with the same toy. And the toddler who has the toy everyone wants is certainly not about to share it."

I laughed and said I'd noticed the same thing when my children were small.

"Adults are the same with money!" he declared. "Everybody wants to be rich, but once we are wealthy we realize the importance of sharing with those less fortunate than ourselves."

"And there is a lot of wealth to share," I said. "It is estimated that the amount of money in the United States that will transfer from one generation to the next before the year 2052 is between $40 and $50 trillion."

"Let me tell you," he replied. "This extraordinary amount of money demands and deserves careful planning and education. We care not just about the transfer of our property, but also the transfer of our personal values."

"How is this best accomplished?" I wondered.

Mr. Howe was not without some sage advice on this one. He said, "First you need to carefully educate your children and grandchildren about the importance of maintaining their current lifestyle no matter how much wealth they may receive. Even very wealthy people admit to deep-seated worries that they may not have enough to achieve all their financial goals and remain financially independent."

"Good point," I said. "I've noticed that one major obstacle to effective planning is the gap between the perception of wealth and the reality of wealth. Some people live beyond their means because they presume they are wealthier than they actually are."

"But always taking out of the meal tub and never putting in soon comes to the bottom," he said, quoting Benjamin Franklin.

"Mr. Howe, are you saying that no matter how much money you have, you should always live within your means and forget about trying to impress your neighbors?"

"That is exactly what I am saying," he replied. "In order to live within your means you need to clearly define what is required to maintain your current lifestyle. That way, as you get older, the additional money you acquire is not automatically spent."

I agreed and said I often help clients approach this by identifying the amount of net annual income they need for personal consumption and maintaining the usual material assets such as home, car, property, and vacation home. Then they need to identify the amount of money they need to maintain their financial independence, future investment, and spending assumptions. It is important for them to explore how these assumptions will impact their ability to maintain their lifestyle.

"Yes, exactly," he responded. "One method a person could use in determining the money required for lifestyle maintenance is establishing a savings account and adding enough money each year to maintain its current value over time. Anything more than this amount is available for current gifting purposes to family, friends, and charity. If I understand my research combined with what you have told me, then gifts to charity may allow for both current income tax and future estate tax savings."

Mr. Howe had strong opinions in the area of maintaining a low-key, economical lifestyle. He encouraged people to be frugal. He told me, "Being frugal will enable you and your children to be self-reliant. Only by being frugal can you hope to take financial control of your life and concentrate on two of the most important aspects of living: things of the Spirit and things of the intellect."

In a fatherly tone he advised me, "Live modestly, regardless of your income. Avoid making a statement with money, especially money you haven't worked for or earned yourself."

He then pointed out, "You should seek to cultivate colleagues, friends, acquaintances, and family that hold similar sound values to yours. Sound values include the traditional values of honesty, integrity, sincerity, reliability, respectfulness, trustworthiness, loyalty, courtesy, kindliness, and service to others." He was not standing on a soap box, but he might as well have been.

"Success in any field, as well as in life, is related to your talent, creativity, and discipline," he said. "Of these three attributes, discipline is the hardest to achieve and maintain. Discipline requires continuous hard work so that you have the skill, knowledge, and perseverance to continue to do what is necessary and right. It is critical to have discipline, even under difficult conditions of fatigue, frustration, outside pressures, time deadlines, and conflicting goals."

Clearing his throat, he continued, "Both my father and grandfather emphasized that nothing succeeds like success. They would tell me that continual successes, even little ones, are likely to lead to later, and possibly larger, successes. You should continuously strive for little successes."

Wealth Transfer to Heirs

"Tell me, Mr. Howe," I asked. "How do you approach this matter of how much to leave to your children and grandchildren?"

Mr. Howe sat quietly, eyes looking toward the ceiling and stroking his chin with the thumb and knuckle of the index finger on his right hand. He then looked down and began shaking his head from side to side.

"Well, you are right," he finally said. "With all the wealth in our country, that is a difficult question to answer. You want to assure your children and grandchildren are safe and comfortable, to help them become established and successful in life, and to provide for their medical or housing needs. You may want them to exhibit character, mental strength, integrity, a sense of family legacy, and responsible behavior—all attributes money cannot buy. However, you do not want to give them too much to cause them harm. You want your heirs to be self-supporting, yet in a position to help others. Achieving this balance is tricky business."

Mr. Howe had my undivided attention. I have been grappling with this issue and wanted to understand more. I inquired, "How have other people approached this issue?"

He sat with his right leg crossed over his left leg, his foot kicking in the air repeatedly when he said, "I read where Bill Gates said, 'One thing is for sure, I won't leave a lot of money to my heirs because I don't think it would be good for them.' He said he would leave each of his children $10 million. While $10 million seems like a lot of money, based on his net worth at the time of $82 billion, $10 million is slightly larger than 1/100 of 1%. This is like someone with $1 million giving a child $100."

Still repeatedly kicking his foot in the air, Mr. Howe continued, "In my view, you must first decide how much money is enough for your heirs. This involves determining how much money will assist and encourage them to become self-sufficient, yet not ruin their desire for personal achievement. This is the fundamental principle that I desire for the grants from my foundation. I don't want my grants used just to provide handouts, but to support programs and activities that help people to become self-sufficient, independent, contributing members of society."

"I remember that, Mr. Howe," I jumped in. "Those are the exact words we put in the charitable purpose of your foundation."

He took a few more air-kicks and continued, "Defining an appropriate inheritance requires careful consideration about each individual child or grandchild. What is appropriate for one may not be appropriate for another. Your task is to identify specific lifestyle attributes you would like your children and grandchildren to enjoy, resulting from receiving an inheritance."

Mr. Howe stopped kicking his foot in the air, uncrossed his legs, sat straight up in his chair, looked intently at me, and said, "Assets you are not allowed to keep or pass on to your heirs are referred to as social capital…."

"Is that because those assets need to be used for the public good of all people?" I interjected.

"Stop interrupting me!" he commanded, then continued. "Social capital is either *involuntarily* extracted from your estate through taxes, or you *voluntarily* contribute them as charitable gifts. Understanding this concept expands the role of philanthropy in planning your estate. Incorporating charitable strategies nearly always make more sense than tax payments in the decision-making process.

"In addition, social capital provides future generations opportunities for personal growth, community service, and wealth management training by exercising responsibility for their family capital through charitable giving.

"Your job is to work with your advisors to explore and define your charitable values and objectives as an integral part of the overall financial and estate planning effort."

Not wanting to get in trouble again, I waited in silence, but Mr. Howe had apparently reached the end of that thought, so I asked, "How much is *enough*?"

How Much Is Enough?

"Well," he reported, "Warren Buffett said the perfect amount to leave children is enough so they would feel they could do anything, but not so much that they could do nothing."

"Brilliant!" I replied. "Then how do I specifically determine that guiding principle in dollars and cents?"

Mr. Howe gave me that wry smile of his and said, "You must design the distribution of your assets so money does not stop the fulfillment of the non-financial objectives you have for your heirs. Some of the questions you need to answer when establishing your financial and estate plan include," he flicked his index finger in the air and continued counting off on the four fingers of both hands the following items:

1. What are my financial *and* non-financial goals for my heirs?
2. Does my financial and estate plan accomplish those goals?
3. What is the best structure to provide my heirs with appropriate assets?
4. Have I provided for unforeseen circumstances?
5. What is the best structure to promote our family values?
6. Are my heirs prepared to act responsibly with the assets I leave them?
7. Will my planning bring my family members closer or pull them apart?
8. Have I made provisions for my community legacy?

"Are you saying, Mr. Howe, that by addressing all of those questions I will be able to design an inheritance plan that will enhance my heirs instead of hindering them?"

"Absolutely," Mr. Howe replied emphatically. "A financial advisor in Texas once told me that the experience of creating capital generally develops personal growth, a sense of achievement, and self-worth. The lack of experience in creating wealth can be dangerous to the recipients of an inheritance."

"How then do I approach determining what to leave my family?"

In short, snappy sentences he retorted, "Determine the amount you wish to give family members during your lifetime. Identify the appropriate amount given to them when you die.

Calculate the amount of tax due on these transfers and establish a reserve to meet that liability.

"The balance of the estate is free for your use in supporting the philanthropic interests of your family, which in turn will reduce the income, estate, and gift tax owed. Many people find that planned giving techniques enable them to accomplish much more than they had anticipated."

"That is terrific advice," I said, and I asked Mr. Howe if he could give me an example of how to do this.

He looked at me and said, "Let's say you want to leave your two children $500,000 each through your estate. Since there currently is no estate tax on $1 million, you will not have to set aside funds to pay the taxes. That means that everything above $1 million is available for your philanthropic legacy.

"However, if there was at the time of your death a $100,000 estate tax on $1 million, then you will have needed to account for that tax in your planning. In that case everything above $1.1 million is available for your philanthropy."

"That makes perfect sense," I said. "And it's easy to figure out as well. Thanks for sharing your ideas with me, Mr. Howe."

Articulating Personal and Family Goals and Values

"Another thing you need to do," Mr. Howe continued, "is to help your advisors ask about your values, community interests, and lessons learned from past involvements. You want your opinions heard, respected, and taken seriously. Since starting your philanthropic profile may be uncomfortable for some advisors, let me share with you a few effective questions to answer for this type of planning. The key is to focus on articulating what you want to accomplish. Are you ready to begin?"

"Yes, Mr. Howe. I'm all set to go," I replied.

He began. "First, ask yourself what principles have guided how you have lived your life, raised your family, or run your business? In other words, what approach has driven your work?" He reached over to my desk, retrieved a legal pad I had lying there, handed it to me and said, "Go ahead—write down your answers."

_____

_____

_____

He waited patiently while I filled up three or four lines and then said, "Now, ask yourself what charitable interests have you pursued as an outgrowth of those values? What type of charitable activities and organizations have attracted you?" He glanced at the legal pad and waited for me to write.

_____

_____

_____

"What have you learned from your giving? What would you do the same or differently?"

_____

_____

_____

"What specific organizations have you been involved with?"

_____

_____

_____

" What are the most important organizations to you and why?"

_____

_____

_____

"What has been the most satisfying charitable gift that you have made in your lifetime? Why?"

_____

_____

_____

"What core values would you like to express through your giving? How would you like to be remembered?"

_____

_____

_____

"Now let's shift gears a little," he said. "When you think about the challenges facing your community, what are your major concerns? List them and ask yourself, 'Should any of these be the focus of my giving?'"

_____
_____
_____

"What would you like to accomplish with your giving? What do you think is possible?"

_____
_____
_____

"How would you like to be involved in, or manage, your giving?"

_____
_____
_____

"What role would you like philanthropy to play in your family? What value would it bring to your children and grandchildren?"

_____
_____
_____

"How much money do you want to commit to charitable giving during your lifetime and how much money after your death?"

_____

_____

_____

This was taking a long time, but I could see the value of it, and with Mr. Howe hunkering over me like a vulture waiting to attack if I made a false move, I kept at it. When I finished answering the last question, he gave a satisfied grunt and said, "Now then, if you can answer all or most of these questions for your advisor, you will be making great progress in your philanthropic planning."

"Thanks, Mr. Howe, for helping me focus on the details of philanthropic planning. Tell me, where do you come up with all this information?"

"Not telling," he said with a grin, "and now I gotta run, but I'll be back next week. Keep your legal pad out."

Chapter 13
Mr. Howe on Planning

Heirs engaged in family philanthropy develop a sense of competency, responsibility, self-worth, and an appreciation for the talents and values of others.
—Mr. EH

I was able to answer all of Mr. Howe's questions in a surprisingly short time period, and then I took my answers home and shared them with my wife. She reminded me of a few additional priorities we share, and before the week was over I was ready for the reappearance of Mr. Howe.

By now my receptionist knew he would likely appear at 10:00 a.m. on Thursday mornings, so she had his English tea at the ready, and she seemed to hardly notice his shabby attire.

What she did notice was the absence of that attire the following week when he showed up in a frumpy brown sport jacket, a double knit tie from the 20th century, and a battered black briefcase.

"My goodness, Mr. Howe!" she exclaimed. "You do clean up well!" He touched his forehead in a polite salute and asked if he could see me.

When we were seated together at a table he snapped open the one working hasp of his briefcase and said, "I have something for you—a design and strategy that you or anybody can use to effectively implement a philanthropic plan."

Philanthropic Design and Implementation

"Look here," he said, pulling out a sheaf of hand-written notes. "You can view wealth in two parts: financial capital and social capital. You have a choice about what you do with each. You can choose to either spend the financial capital during your lifetime or leave it to your heirs. Regarding the social capital, you can either distribute it through voluntary charitable contributions or pay taxes. The most important step in the planning process is to establish clear and concise objectives for both your financial capital and social capital."

To make sure I understood what Mr. Howe had just said, I rephrased it. I said, "In other words, are you saying financial capital is the money I use for the benefit of myself and my heirs, and social capital is the money the government says I must use for the public good?"

"You better write that down before you forget it," he said, so I pulled out the legal pad full of answers to his questions from last week and began taking some notes.

"Ah, good," he said. "By distinguishing financial capital from social capital, you can build a game plan for achieving the objectives of both piles of capital. Hand that over to the right advisor and she will be able to design an appropriate vehicle—or vehicles— to meet your core interests, needs and concerns.

"If you are lucky, she will be astute like Ida Tarbell and therefore able to help you establish a foundation like Mr. Rockefeller—maybe better. She will know to help you address the desired level of involvement you want to retain in managing your philanthropic activities. She will also incorporate the interests, expertise, and desires of your heirs, and take into account your total financial and estate plan in a timely, effective, and tax-efficient manner."

It dawned on me that he was saying back to me much of what I had taught him. I couldn't help but smile to see that the student had become the teacher.

"Many families establish a mechanism for family philanthropy," he was saying. "It might be a special checking account, donor advised fund, Charitable Lead Trust or private foundation. No matter which you choose, the key element is engaging your family. Family philanthropic activity can be a wonderful training ground. Experiences range from understanding due diligence before investments are made, holding others accountable, learning the difference between governance and management, reaching consensus on difficult issues, and feeling positive about doing good for others.

"Heirs engaged in family philanthropy develop a sense of competency, responsibility, self-worth, and an appreciation for the talents and values of others. Family philanthropy offers future generations opportunities for personal growth, community service, and wealth management education."

"I find it interesting, Mr. Howe, that you believe I need to be the one to initiate my philanthropic desires, not my advisors. Why is that?"

Mr. Howe paused like he usually does when I ask a question that he is careful to answer. He crossed his right leg over his left knee and began repeatedly kicking his right foot in the air. Deciding to be blunt he said, "Did you come to me, or did I come to you when it became time for me to establish my foundation like Mr. Rockefeller?"

That said it all, but he continued. "Advisors believe the greatest deterrent to charitable giving is their clients' fear that they will not have enough money to maintain their standard of living and health care needs throughout their lifetimes.

"Most people do not want to be a burden to their families. They want to ensure that they have sufficient funds to meet their needs and not have to rely on children or other family members. They also want to make sure they can provide some type of inheritance for their children and grandchildren.

"Given those concerns, advisors feel uncomfortable bringing up charitable gift planning with clients—because anything given to charity may reduce the client's ability to provide for himself.

"This wouldn't be as big a problem if we all knew when we were going to die," he said bluntly. "But you can get beyond this problem once you've answered the question, how much is enough to leave my heirs? By clearly identifying specific financial targets for personal financial security and the desired amount to pass on to children and grandchildren; you will know the amount you can safely direct to civic purposes."

I asked, "If I should not expect my advisors to initiate such discussions in philanthropic planning, then what *should* I expect from them?"

"You want them to know all about tax and financial planning," he quickly replied. "However, you should also ask for their help in establishing your philanthropic plan. Just don't expect them to initiate the discussion. You are no longer satisfied with 'tools-based' advice focused heavily on the mechanics of giving. Rather, you now need to expect from your advisors opportunities to discuss family values and philanthropic interests and to define the focus of your giving."

I digested this information in silence while he took a sip of now-cold English tea. Then I said, "Let's go back to the idea of involving my family in philanthropy. My children are adults and now live in all parts of the country. How do I make that work?"

"Good question," he retorted. "You see, family dynamics have changed dramatically over the past 100 years. Families have moved from being large in number, as during our agricultural era of the 19th century, to a smaller family size of the 21st century. The average American family household today has 2.55 members as compared to 3.67 members in 1948.

"Another way families have changed is in location. In past generations, many family members lived within walking or short driving distance of each other. A majority of the family members stayed in the same town for their entire lives. As a result, the family targeted their philanthropic focus on the local community. These days children are less likely to stay in the same community where they grew up. Like yours, the average family today has children living in various parts of the country, if not throughout the world. Now we are both more mobile and in many ways more disconnected."

"How does this change impact the way a family carries out its philanthropy?" I asked.

Mr. Howe adjusted his tie and said, "Parents and children may not share as many common interests these days. After kids leave home they become disconnected because of not being an immediate member of the community they grew up. Also, if their parents moved a lot in their quest for better jobs, the children may not feel connected to *any* community.

"So it can be a good thing when your children engage in the philanthropic needs of the place where they currently live. They may have strong desires to use the family foundation to support their own charitable interests. This is an important conversation to have between the children and their parents and grandparents who very likely will wish to continue supporting the community where they worked and raised their family."

I asked. "If there is a conflict in charitable interests between the family generations, how do you best approach the situation?"

"Family feud!" he chuckled, "especially if the family patriarchs insist that all of the philanthropic funds be used to support pre-designated charities. They would like their children to oversee the grants to make certain they are being used wisely and for the desired charitable purposes.

"When the children are not interested in the philanthropic objectives of their older family members, the best way for patriarchs to address this issue is by designating a portion of the annual distributions to charities specified by the younger generation."

"Sounds prudent," I agreed, but I wondered aloud, "What are the potential pitfalls?"

He grinned and slapped his knee, then said, "If your grandma believes pierced ears and tattoos are sinful, she's not going to want you distributing her money to a clinic providing those services to homeless people!"

His example was silly but his point was clear. Your children are not the only people capable of carrying out your wishes. It is ideal when control can remain in the family, but when children and grandchildren disassociate themselves from the family values, they should not be entrusted with the family foundation. In that circumstance, grant-making decisions can be left to non-family members such as trusted advisors, financial institutions, law firms, and community foundations.

"Mr. Howe," I asked, "do you know of an example of a time where the children's grant-making values differed from their parents?"

"I sure do," he quickly replied. "You know, just because something is legal doesn't make it right. That is how I feel about these kids of a former client of mine."

"What did they do that upset you?"

"My client was a very religious man of faith. He went to Mass every week and was successful running his business, being a husband to his wife, and raising three children. They lived in a nice home near my office in Dearborn. His wife predeceased him by a couple of years, and when he died he left a chunk of cash to set up his foundation. His three children were the trustees. He did not restrict the charitable purposes of the grants they could make.

"Well, this fellow and his wife were appalled at the thought of a woman having an abortion. He supported the church annually with his gifts and gave a lot of money to adoption agencies over his lifetime. In fact, it was a surprise to me when I discovered that he did not include adoption charities as a part of his foundation purpose.

"When those kids of his got hold of his money in the foundation, one of the first grants they made was to an organization that helps women get abortions! I know that my client is turning over in his grave at the thought of his hard-earned resources being used in the opposite way he would have designated."

Mr. Howe's face was turning red with anger as he explained, "Because that man left his foundation without any charitable purpose restrictions, his kids can make grants to whomever they like!" In his agitation he began reaching in his pocket for something, realized he wasn't wearing the usual coat, and his hands flailed around until he got control of himself by grasping the two lapels of his brown jacket.

I quickly shifted the topic slightly by saying, "Let's forget about shared values for a minute. Let's talk about how I can teach my children about philanthropic giving." I asked. "I'm not talking about teaching them my values. That is different. How can I teach them about charitable giving?"

"The same way you teach them anything else," he bluntly said. "Just be sure it is one of the things you teach them. For example, start while they're young by giving them an allowance with extra money. In addition to school lunches, toiletries, and other expenses they are responsible for, you can require them to use some of the money to assist someone in need, either directly or through a charity.

"One family gave their two daughters an allowance of $100 each per month. In addition to school lunches, clothing, and other personal care items, each daughter needed to use at least $10 per month to assist another student or charity. This included contributing to an organization such as their church, a food pantry, a homeless shelter, or to their school for a particular educational project. After several years, the daughters were much attuned to various charitable organizations and to people they knew who had specific needs."

"Fantastic!" I said. "What else?"

"Involve your children in the giving process. For holidays such as Thanksgiving, Christmas, New Year's, Easter, or some other special day, you can identify funds the family will distribute to charity as a group. Each family member will bring to the meeting the name of a charity and project where they would like some funds to be given. To prepare for the meeting, they need to research the charity, its needs, and the project and come to the meeting prepared to make a case for why it should receive the family's support."

"I love that idea, Mr. Howe," I said. "You seem to know a lot about educating children on philanthropy."

He looked away with a bit of embarrassment and continued. "You can also take your children to visit charitable organizations and do on-site research when visiting. Going to a children's museum, zoo, aquarium, or planetarium will not only serve as an excellent family outing, but also as a philanthropic educational opportunity for your children.

"Then, when your children become teenagers, teach them about the various scholarship awards for college. This will not only help them understand the scholarship programs available, but they may even apply for and receive such a scholarship for their own education."

Educational Scholarships

"What a great idea," I said. "But are educational scholarships a form of charity?"

"Absolutely! They may be the most common restricted gift in America. I believe there are more gifts made with the educational scholarship restriction than for any other charitable purpose. And they are not given just to traditional colleges and universities, but also to organizations focused on religious education, arts and culture, and health care."

"I'm having a brainstorm," I said in mock seriousness. "Could I make a tax deductible gift to the school where my daughter will attend, designate that gift as a scholarship, and then see to it that my daughter is the scholarship recipient?"

He knew I was joking or else he would have probably slugged me in the shoulder. "That's the problem!" he pronounced. "Because of the potential abuse in providing scholarships to family members, which, by the way, are not charitable contributions, the IRS has developed extensive rules regarding the granting of scholarship awards."

"Tell me those rules, Mr. Howe."

"First," he said, "in order to comply with these rules, there are two primary ways you can set up a foundation to make scholarship awards. The first way is to establish a scholarship program at a qualified public charity. The program can be set up at a school district, college or university, education foundation, or some other organization providing scholarships to students.

"The scholarship program should include specific criteria such as age or year in school, grade-point average, program of study, geographic location, or some other objective criteria that reflects your values.

"In the past, many scholarship programs required the student to demonstrate financial need. Because of the complexities of the financial aid programs today, making awards to students who have financial need may be quite challenging and difficult. With all of the variables that play into determining financial need, sometimes it can be a more subjective than objective process. As a result, many scholarship programs today are staying away from placing the financial need aspect in the criteria."

"That would greatly reduce the complexity of choosing recipients," I said. "Please go on."

"Once you have created your scholarship program at the institution, your foundation can then make grants to the scholarship program you established. You may request permission to be involved as an advisor in the selection process. However, it is the responsibility of the institution to make the scholarship awards to students matching the selection criteria you established.

"The other way your foundation can make scholarship awards is to ask the Commissioner of the Internal Revenue Service for permission to grant scholarship awards directly to students. You will need to ask your legal counsel to prepare an application to the IRS. The application will describe the process your foundation will use to make the scholarship awards."

Mr. Howe leaned back, reached into his vest pocket and retrieved a rather silly looking orange corncob pipe. Assuming the aloof air of an IRS agent, he stuck it in the corner of his mouth and intoned, "The first item you need to identify in the selection process is eligibility. The number of eligible recipients needs to be large enough so there is a wide variety of potential candidates and abuse may be avoided. However, the number also needs to be small enough so everyone eligible can be informed that he or she is eligible."

He shifted the unlit pipe and continued: "For example, if you said you want your foundation to provide scholarship awards to any student in the country demonstrating financial need, the amount of money it would take your foundation to notify eligible recipients could be astronomical. You would spend all your money just on postage! So you will want to narrow down your criteria as much as is reasonable."

"Can you give me a case study?"

"Yes. The Economic Club of Detroit established a scholarship program for students in Wayne, Oakland, and Macomb counties in Michigan. The organization wanted all students in those counties to be eligible to apply for the scholarship.

"Because of the number of eligible students, they required that all applicants be nominated by the students' guidance counselor. Each year, the scholarship program administrator sent the application to all guidance counselors in all public and private schools in these three counties. That satisfied the notification requirement efficiently and at a modest cost.

"You will also need to create the objective criteria used to make the scholarship awards. The criteria can be similar to the items you would include in any scholarship program."

"Is that all?" I wondered. "I mean, we're dealing with the IRS, and that is seldom simple...."

"Right," he quickly replied. "Your application to

the IRS to award scholarships from your foundation will also need to include a description of the selection process. You will need to identify the make-up of a selection committee. That committee must include several educators or persons familiar with the purpose for which students are being educated. The committee must also include other individuals not connected with the foundation, such as community leaders. And the majority of the selection committee members must be persons from outside of the foundation. All this is to make sure there's no hanky-panky going on at your foundation!"

"Hanky-panky?"

"You know," he retorted. "We don't want foundation officers giving scholarships to their own children and grandchildren. That would not be right.

"Finally, you will need to determine if your scholarship will be one-time only or renewable. If the awards are renewable, you will need to determine how long a person has to complete their educational program relative to the renewal process of the scholarship award.

"Once the IRS approves your foundation's request, you may begin implementing the application and selection process as you have disclosed to the IRS."

I said, "I see that while it is possible, it is quite complex to give scholarships directly to students. Wouldn't it achieve the same objective but be a lot easier to simply set up a scholarship program at an existing institution with the selection criteria I want, and then let them select the scholarship recipients and make the awards?"

"For sure," Mr. Howe replied. "The reality is that it may be far easier, less costly, and more effective to work with existing charities to make the scholarship awards."

With that, he tucked his well-chewed corn cob pipe back into his vest pocket and bid me good day.

Chapter 14
Changing Times, Changing Needs

There is certainly an art to planning for a future that can't be known in the present. —Mr. EH

I then spent some time speaking with Mr. Howe about his view on how communities change over time and the significance that can play in philanthropy. Within 50 or so years, some communities go through a total makeover of their commerce, industry, jobs, and demographic makeup. New technologies surface and change the landscape of industry. Big companies close plants and job opportunities change.

"You grew up in the Detroit area, Mr. Howe. How has Detroit changed during your lifetime?" I asked.

"Goodness!" he said. "In the 1960s the city was booming with nearly 1.7 million people. Detroit has 138 square miles of land, but even so, as a result of the 1967 racial riots that took place, a large majority of the population moved out of the city and into the suburbs. The city population has declined by a million people and now has just over 700,000 people.

"Detroit is now in a great urban dilemma with thousands of vacant homes, commercial buildings, factories, and other litter-strewn properties. Crime is up, property values are down dramatically, police and fire security is a vast and underfunded challenge. And even with many square miles of empty houses, homelessness is a huge problem."

I asked him, "Would you agree that as communities change, so do the needs of the nonprofit organizations that emerge to meet those needs?"

"Absolutely," he exclaimed. "Let me give you a great example. There is a community development corporation called Central Detroit Christian (CDC) which works in the low-income community of central Detroit. They report that the area they serve is considered one of the lowest economic zip code areas in the United States."

"Wow," I blurted. "I knew things were tough in Detroit, but didn't realize it was that bad!"

Mr. Howe continued. "In an effort to attack the poverty level, CDC developed a produce market where people can purchase healthy fruits and vegetables. They also allow people from the neighborhood to sell, on consignment, fruits, and vegetables that they grow in the back yards and vacant lots of the neighborhood. They even have a truck that drives around like an ice cream truck selling fresh produce."

"Cool," I commented. "How effective has the produce market been?"

"They received recognition from the State of Michigan and the White House for their work in creating an effective model that provides healthy food to residents in urban communities," stated Mr. Howe. "America's First Lady even visited the market!"

"What else is CDC doing?"

"With all of the dilapidated buildings, people need materials to fix them up. So they created 'Restoration Warehouse' where local residents can purchase building materials at a low administrative cost to fix up and renovate their properties. CDC also developed a landscape company that provides job training for community residents. This project beautifies the neighborhoods while also developing skills as participants become employable, contributing members of society.

"Then too, CDC created a local diner where I eat sometimes. They train cooks and servers who can secure jobs in for-profit companies or create their own businesses.

"In an effort to help children and their families, CDC developed a Saturday morning tutoring program for children. They say their next project is to develop affordable housing and a local Laundromat."

"You know, Mr. Howe, in 1960 no one would have ever dreamed that such needs would exist in the Motor City!"

"That's so true," he replied. "Ironically, the geographic area that Central Detroit Christian Development Corporation serves is adjacent to the former General Motors world headquarters where in the 1950s and 60s the residents were doing very well and the area was thriving."

I wondered aloud, "What other organizations are working to help revitalize Detroit?"

Mr. Howe said, "The Michigan State University College of Law has developed a legal clinic within the city of Detroit. The clinic helps residents apply for changes to the zoning classification of their property.

"With all of the vacant buildings and land, many consumers are purchasing plots of adjacent land for as little as $100 for a plot and then requesting a zoning change from residential to agriculture. As a result, farms are surfacing within the urban sprawl. The landscape of Detroit will look very different 20 years from now compared to how it looked 40 years ago. As the city changes, so do the needs of its residents."

"What is the lesson to be learned here?"

Mr. Howe began rubbing his hands together as though he was washing them but without the soap and water. "If you create your foundation within the current perspective of your community, you may saddle your successors with a philanthropic vision that is impractical to carry out. Instead, why not develop a philanthropic vision broad enough to withstand the changing times?

"An example of this broader vision comes from the story of Samuel and Margaret H. Camp. The Camps owned a company in Jackson, Michigan, in the 1930s and early '40s. They were very community minded and well respected by everyone.

"One winter night in 1944, they were walking to attend a performance of the Jackson Symphony Orchestra at the high school. It was a snowy evening and a car ran out of control, hitting and killing them both. Fortunately, in 1943 they had met with an attorney and finalized their estate plans.

"The plans established several trusts to benefit

family members and their church over the next 68 years. They also included language in the document to ensure that once family members benefited, a certain percentage of the trust would then support charitable organizations and activities that serve the residents of Jackson County, as determined by the board of directors of the local bank.

"These philanthropists knew that over the years the needs and organizations to meet them would change. So, they established a broad philanthropic vision in order to achieve their goal. They also knew that members of a bank board in a local community are typically some of the key leaders who would likely have their fingers on the pulse of both the local needs and existing resources.

"The Camps understood that people holding the bank board positions would be in the best position to wisely distribute their philanthropic dollars in perpetuity."

"They were smart people!" I agreed. "As local business owners they understood how things operate and who is best able to make wise decisions on their behalf."

"But they had a broad vision," he pointed out. "You may have a narrower and limited philanthropic goal. That is not a bad thing, but you need to recognize that your restrictions may cause difficulty in achieving your goal over the long term.

"Consider the American Lung Association (ALA) established in 1904 with the mission to cure tuberculosis and lung disease. For many years, the organization worked to eradicate tuberculosis in the

United States. Once they achieved the mission, they went on to address new initiatives such as clean air, smoking, and other lung-related conditions.

"It's great that they achieved their original mission and purpose. However, now that the mission is achieved, how will the substantial endowment funds be used? Rarely do people anticipate such success, and as a result they fail to outline in their legal documents what to do with the financial resources once the original charitable mission has been achieved."

I was dumbfounded that Mr. Howe understood so much about philanthropic planning. It was as if he didn't need my help to set up his foundation so much as I needed his wisdom, guidance, and counsel on these charitable gift-planning matters and considerations.

Sitting like a wise professor in front of his class, Mr. Howe went on with his lesson: "Consider working with an independent, third-party fiduciary if you care more about achieving a specific mission over benefiting a specific charity regardless of its charitable mission."

"A third-party fiduciary?" I asked.

Wiping his nose with his right coat sleeve, Mr. Howe followed my cue by saying, "Sure. The third-party fiduciary can direct funds to the charity currently addressing the issue that concerns you, but it also has the flexibility to direct funds to new organizations that may be created to address the mission. The new entities that did not exist when you created your fund may prove better able to achieve your objectives. And, when the mission is achieved, the independent overseer may direct the funds to other charitable purposes that you previously identified in the governing documents."

"What a great idea," I noted. "No doubt you have a case study to help me understand how this works."

"Yes, actually, there is a situation that I am familiar with," responded Mr. Howe. "James R. Slade was a businessman and a friend to the chief administrator of a small hospital in a rural Midwestern community. Together they envisioned establishing a hospital unit for Alzheimer's patients. Alzheimer's had affected Mr. Slade's wife, Mary Ann Slade, and he desired to help others with the debilitating disease.

"In his estate plan Mr. Slade established the James R. and Mary Ann Slade Charitable Trust designated to support Alzheimer's patients in the small, rural Midwestern hospital. The problem was that for years the hospital provided no such services. It was always their intention to establish such programs, but they had not yet done so. In the interim, the trust supported other organizations that helped Alzheimer's patients and their families.

"During this interim period, the hospital was sold to a for-profit medical corporation. The same charity that previously owned the hospital used the sale proceeds to create a nonprofit retirement community. As successors to the hospital, the retirement community leadership contacted the trustee of the charitable trust to learn if trust funds could be used to create and operate an Alzheimer's unit in the retirement community. The two parties met and established a plan for achieving Mr. Slade's original desire to help Alzheimer's patients."

"Well done!" I exclaimed.

"Now then," Mr. Howe continued. "If Mr. Slade had given the original funds to the hospital instead of to the trust, would they have ever been used to create an Alzheimer's unit? The Alzheimer's gift restriction on the funds could have easily disappeared during the sale of the hospital and the transition to the retirement community. However, because Mr. Slade had created his foundation like Mr. Rockefeller and me, the funds were used to support Alzheimer's patients in the retirement community, as successor to the hospital that he and his friend had envisioned from the outset."

"There is certainly an art to planning for a future that can't be known in the present," I said. "Mr. Slade pulled that one off brilliantly. I appreciate you bringing this to my attention as it will help me assist people more effectively."

"Make sure you include that one in your book," he said.

This was his second reference to my non-existent book, but I jovially said, "Sure. In fact, it probably deserves an entire chapter."

A very future-minded man, Mr. Howe continued in a serious tone: "Because needs change over time, the number of nonprofit organizations keeps expanding. An organization formed to address a particular need at the time may cease to exist when the need is met, or becomes obsolete. Do you know there were nearly 270,000 nonprofit organizations in 2010? That's two-and-a-half times more than existed in 1985. This is why I want my foundation to be as flexible as possible while still targeting homelessness as its charitable purpose."

I inquired, "Mr. Howe, tell me this: How do you decide when to leave your legacy to a specific charitable organization or when to entrust it to a third-party fiduciary."

I could see the wheels turning inside his head. He bit his bottom lip for a few seconds and then responded: "Your primary concerns should be that of trust and purpose. Do you trust a specific charitable organization with your funds? Do you want to benefit them even if their mission changes over time? If the answer is yes, then you will need to discern if the organization has the capacity to handle the funds and maintain the integrity of the funds over many years."

"No doubt you have a story to go with this?" I prompted.

He nodded and said, "Take what happened to the Charles and Marie Robertson Foundation. Mr. and Mrs. Robertson created the foundation in 1961 with a $35 million bequest. Mrs. Robertson's grandfather, George Hartford, co-founded the Great Atlantic and Pacific Tea Company (A & P Supermarkets). The foundation, created as a trust, supported the Woodrow Wilson School of Public and International Affairs at Princeton University.

"The purpose of the foundation was to support the school and provide a place where men and women who are dedicated to public service may prepare themselves for careers in government service, with particular emphasis on the education of such persons for careers with the federal government that are concerned with international relations and affairs.

"The governance of the foundation required a majority of the board to be representatives from the university and the minority from the Robertson family. The foundation has grown in size to more than $900 million, providing grants totaling more than $27 million per year. Mrs. Robertson passed away in 1972 and Mr. Robertson in 1981.

The year Mrs. Robertson died, Mr. Robertson sent a letter to Princeton University stating that he was unhappy with the low number of Foreign Service graduates from the Woodrow Wilson School. Princeton responded that the world had changed and the private sector is now providing many of the Foreign Service positions within the federal government. They also indicated that the percentages would continue to decline.

"As this was occurring, the assets of the foundation grew exponentially and dollars sent to the university from the foundation increased significantly."

"I see a storm brewing," I said.

"Yes. After both Mr. and Mrs. Robertson had died, their son, two daughters, and their first cousin continued to serve as representatives on the foundation governing board. They repeatedly voiced displeasure with the low numbers of Foreign Service students that the school was educating.

"Because of the disproportionate amount of money sent from the foundation to the university relative to the number of students in the school, the family filed a number of claims against Princeton asserting that the university had knowingly and willfully misused funds. They said the university overcharged the foundation for alleged Wilson School expenses, and that the funds used by the university supported goals that had nothing to do with training students for government service. The family asked the court to have the university return $100 million to the foundation, provide them with direct control of the foundation governance and all its investments."

"Those are serious charges," I observed. "How did the University respond?"

"Princeton University claimed that the charitable purpose of the original gift was broader than the family asserted and that the university has documentation from the donors to that effect. They said the foundation board had always acted by consensus throughout the years with family representative trustees voting in the affirmative. The university also reported that a large number of Wilson School alumni went into non-government careers because many government careers had been privatized.

"What do you think about this case?" Mr. Howe asked me. "Had Princeton truly violated the terms of the trust in ways the family asserts? Or is this a simple disagreement in perspectives and definition of donor intent? Is the university sufficiently accountable on their financial records for expenses of the Wilson School? Does Princeton view the foundation as 'the University's money' in that they can use the funds for whatever purposes they desire? Equally, is the family mainly pursuing the power and prestige that comes with controlling a $900 million charitable foundation?"

Mr. Howe finished his question in a high-pitched voice, shrugged his shoulders, and turned his hands up in the air as if to say with his body language, "who knows?"

"What is the rest of the story, Mr. Howe?"

"The case never made it to trial," he said. "In December 2008, the Robertson family and Princeton University agreed on a settlement. Under the agreement, the university reimbursed the family its legal fees and expenses in connection with the litigation process. The Robertson Foundation dissolved and the assets transferred to Princeton University for the continued use of supporting the graduate program.

"Finally, the university transferred $50 million of Robertson Foundation assets to create a new charitable foundation controlled by the family. The new foundation is to support other colleges and universities with scholarship funds and provide funds to recruit, train, and place graduate students to serve the US government, all in keeping with the donors' original intent."

"Let me see if I get it," I recapped. "Obviously, the Robertson family had lost confidence in Princeton University's stewardship of their family's goal to support the training of graduate students to serve the

U.S. government in foreign and international affairs."

"Check," said Mr. Howe, giving me a thumbs-up.

So I continued, "That $50 million settlement sounds like a fair and equitable way to keep with the original intent of Mr. and Mrs. Robertson. Since the dollars grew beyond the need at Princeton, it is obvious that the charity should expand the number of schools that can receive funding in order to keep accomplishing that goal."

Mr. Howe looked at me stoically, nodded his head in agreement with what I was saying, and said, "There's more, but I have to go now. Maybe the theme of 'changing times, changing needs' will require two chapters in your book...."

Chapter 15
Changing Times, Changing Needs II

The question is not whom do you trust, but who do you trust with your money? When you are gone, it is truly not your money any longer. It's your philanthropic vision that can continue to impact the world in meaningful ways throughout the generations.
—Mr. EH

Mr. Howe was back into his usual, multi-pocketed coat when next I saw him, complete with the rubber band around his lower left pant leg. He was primed to talk more about the changing times in which we live, and the changing needs inherent in 21st century life.

"Everything is changing," he said, "yet nothing is changing. Case study: education. Life is all about education, but the way we go about it changes with the times. Before electricity and computers we had no online university degrees, but today Socrates would probably be holding an online forum."

Having delivered his initial volley of wisdom, he settled into a chair and I said, "Tell me more."

"Say you want to fund education," he said. "Make sure you understand the difference between that education and the delivery system on which it is accomplished. In other words, is the charitable purpose that you wish to benefit lasting, or could it change? The content of what you teach, how you teach it, and the technology used to teach it may change, but you always have education.

"You can say the same thing about healthcare, arts and culture, human services, and religious organizations. So ask yourself this: What is important to you, the specific charitable activity or the manner in which you carry out the activity?"

"Good point, Mr. Howe," I said. "And I'm ready for your case study."

Mr. Howe assumed his professorial air and said, "Back in 1987, Sybil B. Herrington left funds to the Metropolitan Opera Theatre (MET) in New York City to underwrite new productions each year. She signed a gift agreement with the MET stating that her funds would support 'at least one new production each season by composers whose works have been the core of the repertory of the MET during its first century; with each such new production to be staged and performed in a traditional manner that is generally faithful to the intentions of the composer and the librettist (the lyricist).'"

"Sounds reasonable," I said.

"Now then, in 2001, funds from the bequest were used to stage a televised performance of Wagner's 'Tristan and Isolde,' a non-traditional production of the traditional opera. Although the funds were used to create a traditional opera, the use of television was considered by the independent overseer of Mrs. Harrington's fund to be not strictly in keeping with the donor intent, so the overseer demanded that the bequest be transferred to another foundation."

"Interesting," I said. "Did the overseer really have Mrs. Harrington's best interest in mind by quickly pulling the trigger and demanding that the funds be yanked from the Opera?"

"That's it," said Mr. Howe. "You have to continually ask, 'What is important to you? Do you want the organization to do the same things always? Or do you want them to be creative and use your funds to be relevant in the changing times?'

He continued. "Sometimes, cultural norms change such that things previously accepted in society are no longer embraced. As a result, future generations may view a restriction to be unacceptable that at one time was a cultural norm.

"That happened to the Tennessee Division of the United Daughters of the Confederacy with their $50,000 gift in 1935 to Vanderbilt University. The gift was to build Confederate Memorial Hall, a dormitory intended to honor individuals and their families who had served in the Confederate Armed Forces during the American Civil War."

"I am not familiar with the Daughters of the Confederacy," I said. "What happened?"

"Well, in October 2002, the university made the decision to remove the word 'Confederate' from the name of the building due to outcries from the Student Government Association. The building name was re-titled 'Memorial Hall.' This action did not sit well with the United Daughters of the Confederacy, and they filed a claim against the university requesting that they not be allowed to remove the word

'Confederate' from the name."

I asked. "How did the Court respond to the claim?"

"The judge ruled in favor of the university," exclaimed Mr. Howe, showing me his ironic grin. "But the judge also ruled the university would have to reimburse the United Daughters of the Confederacy their original $50,000 contribution with interest dating back to 1935. Needless to say, that would have been a lot of money!"

"And then?" I prompted.

"To this day Vanderbilt University has a building named Confederate Memorial Hall!"

I asked, "What do you think is the lesson to be learned from this situation?"

"Just what I was saying—as times change, so do people and cultural norms. It would have been difficult for the United Daughters of the Confederacy to imagine that the university would no longer desire to have the word 'Confederate' as a part of the name on the dormitory. You just have to realize that over the generations, things viewed as acceptable today may take on a different meaning in the future. You need to understand this fact and plan your philanthropy accordingly."

International Grant Making

I was interested in Mr. Howe's thoughts on the future changes that he sees in philanthropy. So, I asked him, "Mr. Howe, how will philanthropy change over the next 100 years?"

He pulled his knees together, placed his elbows

on them, cradled his chin in the palms of his hands and just sat there thinking. In his mind he must have been shuffling a deck of cards, sorting out what to use and what to discard. He must have sat without uttering a word for two or three minutes. I shifted to a more comfortable position and just waited.

"The world is shrinking," he finally said. "We now live in a world without borders. On these streets here in Detroit we have people from all over the planet. And we can go anywhere in a flash. Therefore, we know of global needs. Philanthropy is responding by going to the source of a problem no matter where it exists on Planet Earth. The challenge is no longer with geography or the barriers of oceans or mountains. The challenge is for our government."

This insight took me a bit by surprise, so I just said, "How do you mean?"

"Well, one challenge is determining what public policy should be relative to allowing charitable tax deductions for gifts to foreign charities. Right now you cannot make a gift to a foreign charitable institution and claim that gift as an income tax deduction. However, you can leave a portion of your estate to a charity located outside of the United States, and your estate may claim an estate tax charitable contribution deduction."

"That's strange. It seems like there may have been a compromise on the public policy debate, so they split the difference regarding tax benefits for gifts to foreign charities," I quipped. "One side of the debate said no to charitable deductions and the other side said yes, so they prohibited the income tax deduction but allowed the estate tax deduction."

"You may be right," responded Mr. Howe. "But there is a more serious challenge. A lot of the financial support for terrorist activities around the world is laundered through legal international foundations, and this is obviously of concern for the United States government. The IRS has developed policies and requirements for private foundations and other organizations making international grants. If you want your charitable foundation involved in international grant making, there are some policies which you will need to consider and adhere to."

"What are some of those policies, Mr. Howe?"

"First, you will need to make sure that the charitable purposes of the international grant and organization are consistent with those of your foundation. The governing documents of your foundation must allow you to make such international grants. If they state, for example, that you may only make grants to charitable organizations domiciled in the United States, then you will have to change and expand the purposes of your foundation before making the grant."

"I would have never thought of that," I commented. "What are some other policies?"

"You will also have to administer a policy known as the 'equivalency determination.' Using reasonable judgment and making a good-faith determination based on an affidavit signed by the international charity grantee, you will need to determine if the organization would qualify as a public charity if located in the United States. Completing such an affidavit certificate of tax-exempt status signed by the international charitable grantee will provide a good checklist that the organization agrees to in helping ensure that the activities are consistent with public policy of the United States. You will also need to require that the organization provide your foundation with a report on the specific use of the funds.

"In addition, you cannot make grants to foreign governments. However, you can make grants to agencies created by a foreign government that support specific charitable purposes such as disaster relief, schools, hospitals, and orphan homes."

"This is getting complex," I observed.

"There is more," he replied. "In order for your foundation to make international grants, the country and organization you wish to make the grant to must not be listed on the Office of Foreign Assets and Control (OFAC) list. This list, published by the U.S. Government, includes all persons and organizations suspected of terrorist or money-laundering activities.

"The grantee organization will need to provide you with a list of its governing board members, financial statements, and a description of their charitable activities, often published in some type of annual report.

"Finally, the organization will need to assure you that there will be no private benefit or use of your foundation's grant funds by individuals, corporations, or organizations affiliated with the charity."

I said, "Thank you, Mr. Howe. I am beginning to see exactly how philanthropy will get even more complex as the world becomes smaller."

"Complex, yes. But not impossible," he exclaimed. "You will just want to be sure your funds are used for the intended charitable purposes and not captured unknowingly by illegal activity or government corruption."

"How can you do that when you are so far from the charity?" I asked.

"One way to assist you in such due diligence is the use of a third-party Non-Government Organization," he replied. "An NGO is authorized to work in a particular country and will have staff on the ground that can make certain your funds are used appropriately. Another way an NGO can assist is by helping you understand the cultural view of a particular situation. What is acceptable in another country may not necessarily be appropriate in the United States."

"Do you have experience with this?" I wondered.

"Of course," he said. "There are examples within a block of here. Immigrants come here to overcome some of these differences. For example, what is paid for labor on a project may be much less in the country of the grantee than in the United States. To overpay for labor, although generous, may cause a problem with the local residents of the country you seek to assist with your grant. In some cases, you may end up not making grants for needed charitable purposes because you do not understand the practices and philosophies of a particular culture."

Sunset Provisions

Mr. Howe spent several minutes gazing out over the horizon, then looked at me eye-to-eye, and said, "Given the fact that times change, communities change, and needs change, you may want to consider including a 'sunset' provision for your foundation. This provision requires your foundation to terminate and distribute all of the assets to charitable organizations at some point in the future."

"If someone wanted to do that," I asked, "why wouldn't they simply given away all of the money to charity in the first place rather than setting up a foundation?"

Mr. Howe responded in a calm, calculated manner. "If you include such a provision, you will find yourself asking the same fundamental questions you wrestled with to establish your foundation. Whether your foundation continues in perpetuity or terminates, you will need to come to grips with the question of whom to trust with your philanthropic vision.

"Notice that the question is not whom do you trust, but who do you trust with your money? When you are gone, it is truly not your money any longer. It's your philanthropic vision that can continue to impact the world in meaningful ways throughout the generations."

"That's pretty smart thinking, Mr. Howe," I stated. "What is the best way to approach this issue?"

He posed, "You will need to determine who you want to involve in succession planning for your foundation, and how many generations you want it to operate. Many people today are placing sunset provisions into their governing documents. These provisions state that on specific date, or when a certain generation is no longer able or willing to serve, the foundation will disband and all the assets be distributed to charitable organizations.

"For example, I understand that Warren Buffett has committed all of his personal assets—worth many billions of dollars—to the Bill and Melinda Gates Foundation. Together, Mr. Buffett and Mr. and Mrs. Gates decided that the foundation should terminate in the year 2050. Imagine how much money will be granted over the next 40 years to charity!

"Along with your sunset provision, you may want to consider including directions on how to implement the dissolution of the foundation. One challenge of these termination clauses is the implementation process. You definitely want to avoid waiting until the termination date to begin distributing the funds. In that situation, properly distributing all of the assets could be difficult."

"I see another problem," I ventured. "The usual charities receiving funds might get a large sum at once and not handle it properly."

"Yes, and that's another reason for the sunset provision including a gradual dissolution process. If the organizations receiving funding know the foundation is terminating, they may feel they do not need to be as accountable to the programs in which they are requesting funding since the foundation must make the distributions regardless.

"Also, as you suggest, the organizations may not be ready to receive the amount of grant dollars that the foundation will contribute to them in order to divest itself of all of its assets. If that were to happen, the primary reason for placing a termination clause on the foundation in the first place may be hindered."

I asked, "What is the fundamental reason philanthropists wish to include termination clauses in their foundation documents?"

"Generally speaking, they do not want their money to outlast their charitable vision and then get used inappropriately later. They want the funds distributed to the right charities and used as directed. But if the amount of funds distributed is significantly large, the charities will not be able to use all of the funds for their purposes either. In that case, the foundation's assets end up sitting in the organization's endowment instead of remaining in the foundation's active accounts.

"Either way, the assets exist for future use and benefit of the charitable mission. When that does become the case, the next thing I wonder about is this: How can I know they have the infrastructure and are in a position to properly manage those funds over the long-term?"

"Yes, how can you know that?" I asked.

"You can't," he said. "You can't know the future. You can just use your best judgment and use your money the best way you know how to accomplish all the good you can."

"You have given me a lot to wonder about," I said. "But taking all these eventualities into account, what is a good rule of thumb when it comes to establishing a sunset provision?"

Mr. Howe blinked his eyes a few times and then said, "There isn't a rule of thumb. It's entirely up to you. But if you do decide to include a sunset provision, make sure you also specify the number of years prior to the termination date to begin distributing the assets and not leave it all for the deadline.

"This will allow your foundation managers to grant the funds strategically to charitable organizations that can handle the large distributions as well as ensure that their programs and activities are enhanced for the community good."

I said, "Your foundation is to help homeless people in Detroit. What if the day comes when there are no homeless people?"

Mr. Howe said, "The poor you will always have with you."

Chapter 16
Follow the Vision

The leadership does not have a compelling long-term vision. Therefore, they only attract the amount of resources that is commensurate with their short-sighted vision. —Mr. EH

Mr. Howe and I sat quietly on the front porch of one of the many abandoned homes on the east side of Detroit where he had invited me to meet him. By now I trusted this street-savvy man and felt comfortable entering his world. He had reached into one of the pockets on the left side of his coat and pulled out a tape measure. He began repeatedly pulling the tape out and releasing it so that it recoiled back into the housing. Constantly snapping the tape in and out, he began his class for the day.

"Earlier we discussed how much money Americans have compared to the rest of the world. Because there are so many resources in our country, the philanthropy and charitable nonprofit sector in America is far more advanced than in other parts of the world.

"In other places, most charitable work involves helping people with their most basic needs: food, shelter, and clothing. Instead of simply focusing our attention on food pantries, orphans, healthcare, education, church, religious organizations, libraries, literacy, arts, culture, homelessness, science museums, and other types of human service agencies, we have taken our charitable giving to the next level," he observed.

"We have?" I said.

He replied, "We have Save the Whales! We have Save the Elephants, Cheetahs, and Lions! We have charitable organizations to preserve our lands and parks. We have funds for research to cure illnesses, and to protect and preserve wild sheep, ducks, and other species. These causes are not bad, they just illustrate the vast resources we have to extend beyond traditional charity to address issues more peripheral to basic human needs.

"The typical nonprofit organization in America generally has enough resources to meet its current needs and achieve its immediate vision. Yes, there are enough funds available to meet all of the charitable needs in the country—and I mean funds from private sector philanthropy, not government taxes and support," he exclaimed.

"What evidence is there for believing that?" I wondered.

He pulled his tape measure out about three feet, let it zip back into itself and said, "Notice that I said 'immediate vision,' not long-term vision. The problem is that most nonprofit organizations do not have a big enough vision to attract the resources to meet all of the needs they attempt to address. They settle for achieving less because they do not have the funding to do more. Their long-term view fits their current level of funding."

I observed, "Are you saying they have the same hand-to-mouth mentality as your homeless friends?"

"Precisely! The leadership does not have a compelling long-term vision. Therefore, they only attract the amount of resources that is commensurate with their short-sighted vision."

I jolted upright and said, "Is that your plan? You want to help me and all those charities the same way you want to help homeless people—by giving us a vision for bigger things?"

He put his tape measure down on the porch floor and said, "Have I ever told you about SpringHill Camp? It is a youth serving, Christian-based organization headquartered in Evart, Michigan. SpringHill does an amazing job providing outstanding camp experiences for youths of all ages. They have excellent main campus facilities in the small town of Evart where they provide summer campers with fantastic experiences. They also provide weekend camp experiences for church youth groups and families in the winter months, which include winter activities such as snow-tubing and ice-skating.

"SpringHill also expanded by opening a campus in southern Indiana. The Indiana campus allows them to serve children, youth, and families in a different geographic location. SpringHill offers high-quality programming. To achieve this, they need the resources to pay highly competent, qualified, and creative staff. They provide first-rate equipment and facilities and excellent accommodations."

I had to interrupt him: "What makes SpringHill different, Mr. Howe?"

He smiled inwardly and I could see that what he was about to say touched him deeply: "Recently, SpringHill expanded its programming to offer day camps in urban and suburban communities. These camps work through contracts with churches to run neighborhood camps for a week. They bring in climbing walls, ropes courses, waterslides, and other fun activities.

"SpringHill also provides all of the staffing. This allows the church staff and volunteers to spend time with the kids to enjoy them and get to know them better. They do this in southeast Michigan—including Detroit—the greater Chicago area, and throughout northern Indiana.

"Many families in the poor economic communities where SpringHill runs day camps are not able to pay the fee to send their children to camp for a week. So SpringHill raises the funds and provides scholarships to those children. It has been relatively easy for SpringHill to raise scholarship funds because of the tremendous impact a week at day camp has on kids."

"I think I see your point," I said. "SpringHill has a bigger vision than just surviving up there in Evert, Michigan."

"It's even bigger than that," he said. "Their leadership has set a goal to reach annually 260,000 campers by 2025. They are currently serving approximately 55,000 per year. This means they will be expanding and duplicating their day camp model in urban and suburban communities around the country.

"They do not yet have all of the resources they need to achieve the goal. Yet they have set out for the target and will be seeking partners to assist them in reaching over a quarter of a million children each year.

"Their vision is big. Their mission is good. Their service is of great value to our society. I have no doubt they will be able to secure the resources necessary to achieve their goal. That is how they are different!"

"Where is the vision of other organizations?" I followed.

He bent over, picked up the tape measure, and pulled it out just one inch. "This is the length of their vision," he suggested. "They say, when we get the funds, then we will expand our vision.

"But where there is no vision, the project will eventually die. Resources follow vision, not the other way around. Charitable organizations need to cast a vision and then develop a game plan to achieve that vision. They need to execute their plan within the resources they have, yet always keep pushing to get their organization to the next level and closer to a larger goal."

I asked, "Can you pinpoint the difference between SpringHill and these typical organizations?"

He pulled the tape measure all the way out and said, "SpringHill is long on leadership. Leadership is the key difference. They know what Mr. Rockefeller knew—that in order to address all of the needs in our country and around the world, we need organizations with strong leaders."

Mr. Howe continued. "Charitable organizations need to have solid, committed governing board members who see the big picture and can fully support a broader vision. Charities need quality executive staff leadership capable of creating a vision and implementing a plan to achieve it. These executives need to be able to cast that vision in a way that anyone can understand it and know what is required in order to achieve it."

"Why is this such a rare thing?" I inquired.

"Good question," he muttered. "Many nonprofit organizations have board members who want to just micro-manage the staff. Or they define success as a balanced budget. They just have a year-to-year vision, which is really no vision at all.

"They may have another problem, too," he said. "They may have executive staff leaders who are not confident or desirous enough to reach for an expanded vision. Many are too worried about paying the bills today instead of creating a vision that will attract the capital needed to expand the mission as well as meet current expenses. Because of this 'here and now' mentality, most charities have not established a proper infrastructure to manage long-term endowment funds."

Relaxing a bit, Mr. Howe observed, "It is always interesting to see how an organization handles an unexpectedly large bequest. Suppose the charity is living hand-to mouth with little to no reserve funds. Now imagine that all of a sudden, the organization receives word it is the beneficiary of a $2 million bequest."

"There would be dancing in the streets," I suggested.

"Just briefly," he said chuckling. "Then they will immediately form a committee! Assuming the bequest is undesignated and available for general charitable purposes, the committee will discuss all the ways to use the funds. These discussions will generally show you the appalling lack of vision in the organization. Typically, they will earmark the funds for immediate projects, and within several years the funds will be depleted and the organization will have done nothing to strengthen its financial underpinnings and long-term sustainability."

"Just like most of those people who win the lottery," I observed. "What would be a better way to respond to such a windfall?"

"You're getting ahead of me," he said. "Let me tell you a story. I once did some work with a national breast cancer research organization. They brought in a consultant to guide them in raising long-term endowment and reserve funds, and they told him they were in the business of stamping out breast cancer. What they failed to tell the consultant was that 85% - 90% of all funds raised were used merely to pay for the expenses of operating the events that raise the funds! So their fund-raising program was doing little more than merely paying for itself.

"If this same organization were to develop a long-range finance plan that included raising endowment funds, it would be able to cover more of the fundraising costs with the takeout from the endowment. They could then direct more of the dollars raised from the public events each year for actual breast cancer research."

"Let me see if I understand what was really happening," I said. "They *said* their mission was stamping out breast cancer, but in actual fact their main function was merely the survival of their organization. But if they could succeed at raising more long-term funding, then they could do some actual cancer research to achieve the stated mission."

"That's it," said Mr. Howe.

"Okay," I said. "Let's say I have my pile of money together and am ready to leave it to charity. How do I choose which organization receives the funds?"

"Before signing on the dotted line," he said, "pick a favored charity and ask them a few questions. Begin by asking them what role gifts from estates and trusts play in their financing the mission and purpose.

"If they say something like, 'we love receiving those types of gifts—they give us a great jumpstart on next year's operating budget,' then you know they have no long-term finance plan in place.

"Continue by asking them what types of expenses they support with a bequest. How does bequest income help them to achieve their mission and purpose? If you receive general and not specific responses, it typically means the organization has not thought much about the question and may not have the structure in place to properly steward your bequest."

"What else should I ask?" I interjected.

"Ask about their capacity to achieve their vision," he continued. "If they have the resources, do they have the capacity and the plan to achieve the long-term mission and vision?

"The charity may also need to shape its mission to be more results-oriented, like SpringHill Camps. Their results-oriented mission is simple: To annually reach 260,000 campers by 2025. It is tangible, measurable, and focused on the core mission of the organization."

As Mr. Howe dropped the tape measure back into his pocket, he said, "The bottom line is this: The nonprofit organization should not exist just to perpetuate the jobs of the staff. It should be mission-focused, continually striving to meet the needs of the constituency it exists to serve."

Endowment Fund Basics

"Mr. Howe," I said. "This conversation leads me to believe that an endowment fund must be very valuable to the organization that meets the criteria you have identified. Talk to me about why I should consider contributing to such a fund on behalf of the charity I care about."

He took an apple out of his pocket and began to polish it on his knee. "The most important thing to remember about endowment funds," he began, "is that they generally come from a donor's accumulated wealth. Since many charitable organizations have tunnel vision regarding the 'here and now,' they tend to seek current operating funds from their donors' disposable income. As a result, they miss out on receiving substantial gifts from the donors' trusts and estates.

"Once the organization takes a longer financial view and begins pushing to create an endowment, that opens the door to an entirely new source of funding from the same constituency."

He paused to take a bite of the apple, so I said, "Please define exactly what you mean by an endowment fund, Mr. Howe."

Juice squirted from his lips as he said, "The law defines an endowment as funds not immediately expendable. It might be a perpetual fund to provide an ongoing stream of income to the organization, or a fund that is entirely distributed over a specified time period for various capital projects.

"Most endowment funds play a key role in providing the long-term financial stability of nonprofit organizations."

He spit an apple seed on the porch floor and said, "Now remember—there are three primary ways an endowment fund helps a charity.

"First, an endowment provides an annual stream of income that affords a stable operating budget for the organization. That's especially valuable during tough economic times.

"Second, an endowment can provide an annual stream of funds for working capital to start new programs or expand existing ones. As times and needs change, charitable organizations need to fine-tune their programs and ways they carry out their mission. Having some working capital from an endowment for such activity is essential for the long-term sustainability of a charitable organization.

"Third—and this is more important than most people think—an endowment fund at an organization creates a model for others to emulate."

"Emulate?" I asked.

He was eating the apple, core and all, and he spit another seed on the porch floor before saying, "How is the younger generation going to learn about their responsibility to help others if charitable organizations do not inform them of whom and where the endowment funds came from?

"How can these kids know what to do if they have not heard about people like Mr. Rockefeller and other people who sacrificed to make things better for those who came after them? That is what it means to emulate!"

I said, "So the charity with an endowment should not keep it a secret?"

It was as if he had been hit by a bolt of lightning. He jolted straight up and shouted, "Absolutely not! Tell everybody about it! The donors of endowment funds are the superheroes! Everyone should want to be like them.

"Put their pictures on the wall! Write articles about them! Publish pamphlets describing the various funds created, their charitable purposes, and the impact on the organization the funds have had. All of these ideas are easy and cheap to do, and probably the best investment a charitable organization can make to stimulate additional giving to their endowment fund."

I said, "It all comes down to vision, doesn't it, Mr. Howe? Smart donors will follow the long-term vision of bold leaders who can see beyond the current fiscal year."

The only thing remaining of his apple was the stem. Mr. Howe tossed it over the porch railing into an ornamental shrub and said, "Uh huh. You've got that right."

Chapter 17
Can They Handle Your Funds?

Has the organization created the kind of management and administrative infrastructure that will enable it to steward your gift well into the future?
—Mr. EH

Let's assume the charity you want to bequeath to has a long-term vision and a well-considered plan to achieve that vision. The next question to ask is whether they can properly handle your bequest. Have they created the kind of management and administrative infrastructure that will enable them to steward your gift well into the future?

I wanted to ask Mr. Howe about this, but he was in failing health and not as punctual as formerly. One day during my lunch hour I was striding toward the pharmacy to pick up a prescription when I saw him on a park bench eating a package of peanut M&Ms. He had opened the top right corner of the package, put a few in his right hand, and was placing them into his mouth one by one as if they were vitamin pills.

I sat down next to him and asked how he was. He responded, but not to my question. "Did you know," he said, "that charitable endowment funds are governed under the Uniform Prudent Management of Institutional Funds Act (UPMIFA)?"

"I did know that," I said. "Each state has slight variations on the general rules."

It was as if he didn't hear me. He kept talking: "Originally created in 1972, the first version of the Uniform Code was known as the Uniform Management of Institutional Funds Act (UMIFA). The original UMIFA defined endowment funds as long-term perpetual funds. The Uniform Code considered the original contribution amount as the historical dollar value of the endowment, similar to the idea of the fund having a cost basis. The law specified that you could not spend any amount below the historical dollar value of the endowment fund. Conversely, you could spend everything above the defined historical amount. If you did that however, you would not provide for any capital appreciation of the fund to keep up with inflation."

"Not many people know about UMIFA, Mr. Howe," I said. "Have you been putting in more time at the public library?"

Pouring a few more peanut M&Ms into his hand, he continued, "In the 1950s and 60s, many alumni created endowed scholarship funds at colleges and universities. If the original contribution amount were $2000, the college would generally use all of the earnings above that amount for the student scholarships. Typically, the annual earnings came to about $50, which at that time provided a nice scholarship for a student.

"The problem occurred when the University used 100% of the earnings each year for 30 years. The scholarship still only had a balance of $2000, still generating $50 per year. But by the 1980s, $50 could barely purchase one book, let alone help pay for tuition and fees.

"That's when many institutions of higher education attempted to eliminate individual endowed scholarship funds and collapse them into one massive pool. From a financial management point of view, this made perfect sense. However, the plan did nothing to preserve the donor's intent or recognize the family name and the generous commitment they had demonstrated many years before."

I asked, "Did the original UMIFA law foster this short-term management view?"

"Exactly," he exclaimed. "The emphasis of UMIFA was on earnings primarily defined as interest and dividends. To generate as much income as possible, many endowment funds were invested with a high percentage of the assets in fixed income securities. Such securities provide for the cash flow needs of the endowment, but they do not generally appreciate.

"UMIFA also caused difficulty for charitable organizations in terms of annual budgeting. Since income varied from year to year, it made it difficult for charities to plan how much of the endowment would be available for the intended charitable purpose."

"That makes it really tough on the chief financial officers at those organizations," I stated.

"And further," he continued as he bit into another M&M, "Under UMIFA, an endowment fund could not be used if the fund's current market value was below the original contribution amount. If a market correction occurred within the first few years of establishing the endowment fund, the charity was in a conflict between its donor's intent and the law. The donor contributed the funds to help the organization generate support for its mission immediately. However, the law did not permit the organization to do so."

He offered me an M&M, but I said "No thanks," and he continued.

"If a donor establishes an endowment fund with $100,000, it is anticipated that at least $5000 will be available each year to support the charitable purpose of the fund. However, if the investment strategy of the endowment is to generate income for the charitable purposes of the fund and bond values dropped, bringing the market value of the endowment below the original $100,000, the organization could not legally use any of the funds. Situations like this resulted in disgruntled donors and frustrated university administrators."

"Didn't people see what was happening and do something about it?" I asked.

"Yes," replied Mr. Howe. "That is why, in 2006, UPMIFA was drafted. The Uniform Prudent Management of Institutional Funds Act replaced all UMIFA laws, and states adopted the new uniform code with a few variations in each state. However, a number of main points are included in all versions of the law.

"For one thing, the law eliminates the historical dollar value for an endowment fund—a smart change. The law also allows for total return investing.

This means the endowment fund investments can target long-term asset classes such as stocks. So instead of investing just in fixed-income securities, the endowment can diversify and invest for a total return."

"Isn't that more risky?" I wondered.

Mr. Howe replied, "Not really. Although market conditions fluctuate through the years, in total return investing you are looking at the returns of the various investments from a long-term perspective. While fixed-income securities generate income, they do not have nearly the potential to appreciate. Stocks may generate a little income in the form of dividends, but they may also appreciate over time. By strategically setting the percentages of the investments of the endowment funds into a variety of assets, you can generate both income and appreciation of the funds to meet current spending needs as well as growth to offset inflation."

This sounded like a wise strategy, so I quickly asked, "Mr. Howe, what do you think is the optimum asset allocation for an endowment fund?"

He replied, "Studies have shown that the best asset allocation for an endowment fund is to place between 50% and 70% of the investments in equities and 30% to 50% in fixed-income securities. We call this a balanced asset allocation between stocks and bonds, and as I said, the goal is to maintain a consistent return while providing for some appreciation of funds."

Thinking back to what he said about the UPMIFA law, I asked, "What else changed with the new law?"

"Well, for one, the new UPMIFA law allows for an annual take-out of the value of the fund regardless if it has appreciated or not. Some states require the charity use a minimum of two percent of the average fund balance each year for the charitable purpose. Other states have also set a maximum that an organization can remove from an endowment fund at seven percent of the balance in any given year.

"The new UPMIFA law also seeks to help organizations prudently managing their endowment funds to meet the short-term needs of their operating budgets and grow the funds to sustain purchasing power over many years.

"Think again about that $100,000 example I gave you. If you take the same $100,000 endowment fund under the new law and take five percent of its value out each year while investing the fund for long-term growth, over the years the dollar amount of the five percent will increase because of the appreciation of the fund. This will enable the charity to have sufficient funds available to meet their expenses and keep up with inflation."

"Do all endowment funds fall under this law, Mr. Howe?" I inquired. "Or do some charities find a way to get around the requirements?"

"There is a way around the UPMIFA law," he said. "A charity can create its own policies and have donors sign agreements placing the gifts under those policies as they exist today and as may be amended in the future. These policies describe how funds are administered, how much is taken out each year, and how funds are redirected to another charitable purpose if the original purpose is not able to be fulfilled."

"What about the investments?" I asked.

"Same thing," he said. "Charities can also develop their own an Investment Policy Statement, known as the IPS. The IPS creates a roadmap for the investment managers relative to the risk tolerance of the endowment fund. The IPS also describes the spending policy, and that helps the investment managers make sure there are sufficient funds available for use each year."

I asked, "Who should take the initiative to set this up at the charity, Mr. Howe?"

"It's simple," he replied. "The charity's finance or investment committee should hire and oversee the performance of an investment manager, making sure the manager maintains consistency with the investment policy statement. It is the job of the organization's governing board is to hire professionals to invest the funds in a manner consistent with its investment policies."

I quizzed him: "What determines if reserve funds of a charity are permanent endowment and fall under this law, or if they are exempt?"

Mr. Howe was pleased with my question. He replied, "Sometimes there is confusion regarding whether an endowment is classified as permanent or expendable. Only a donor's contributions to an organization's endowment fund may be considered permanent. If a donor does not make a gift with an endowment restriction, or if the organization does not solicit for endowment, then all funds are considered expendable."

"That seems simple enough," I said.

"What sometimes gets confusing," he continued, "is when governing boards take excess funds and place them into the endowment. These funds are not considered part of the permanent endowment. They are classified as board-designated or quasi endowment funds. They manage the funds like permanent endowment and generate annual income for the charitable purposes of the organization.

"However, future boards may enact resolutions to take all of the funds out of the endowment and spend them entirely."

I said, "You have reached the usual place in our conversations where an example would help me understand."

"Yes, most certainly," he responded. "Let's say an organization has a surplus of funds in a given year totaling $250,000. The board designates that money to be placed in endowment and spends only the income generated from that investment. Because that money is considered 'board-designated,' future boards can agree to remove the entire $250,000 plus any growth from the endowment and spend it on its charitable purposes."

"I didn't realize that could happen," I commented.

Continuing to opine, Mr. Howe said, "Another confusing aspect is spending policy. Many people are under the impression that you can only spend the interest and dividends earned each year, but spending all the income each year creates many challenges and pitfalls.

"Best practice is to establish a more conservative spending policy that provides reliable income each year, yet also reinvests some of the income so the principal can grow."

"Is there a good formula for doing that?" I wanted to know.

"Plenty of them," he said. "Suppose the value of an endowment fund on December 31 is $100,000 and it has consistently returned five percent a year. To keep the principal growing, the organization should budget four percent of that amount, or $4,000, to use in its operating budget.

"The challenge is that budgets are calculated well in advance of the calendar year end, and an organization may not be able to predict what the year-end market value will be for its endowment fund. So if the fund returns only three percent and the charity has budgeted four percent, then you have slid into a deficit situation."

Mr. Howe placed the crumpled bag of the few remaining peanut M&Ms into his pocket, and continued. "In order to develop a more predictable approach, some organizations use an average account value. They may be a little under one year but plenty over the next year. The longer the average is used, the more predictable the cash flow becomes. This type of spending policy is excellent for smoothing out the amount of dollars available for use each year and provides predictability in budgeting."

I said, "Doesn't it also grow the fund by means of compound interest?"

"Yes, and that's great until the specified purposes of the fund become obsolete or the charity decides to eliminate the program while plenty of money still remains in the fund."

"The French came up with a way around that problem," I said, and he knew exactly what I was talking about.

"*Cy pres,*" he said. "*Cy pres* is a French legal phrase that means 'closest to or as near as possible.' In other words, the organization can identify a similar charitable purpose that is as 'near as possible' to the donor's original intent.

"Let's say a donor established an endowment fund to support a university's early childhood education program. Due to a variety of circumstances, the organization decides to eliminate the program. Under *cy pres*, they may decide to direct the endowment funds toward something similar— say a new youth education initiative. In any case, the organization needs to have a process in place for making such a change."

"What if the organization does not have a clue about exercising this type of change in charitable purpose?" I wondered.

Mr. Howe said, "Then state law will prevail. Most states have enacted *cy pres* laws that work similarly to the UPMIFA law in terms of their oversight and governance over endowment funds. Charities should be certain to include such *cy pres* language in their endowment fund policies to give donors peace of mind, knowing how the organization will adjust the charitable purpose, should the need arise."

Institutional Memory

"That's a great point, Mr. Howe," I said. "At the time of making the gift, many donors are excited at the thrill of being generous. They do not always pause to ask the types of issues that you have mentioned."

"There's more," he said, prying a small box of jellybeans from his pocket and placing one into his mouth. "If you find yourself negotiating a major gift with a nonprofit organization, you will need to discern how much institutional memory the organization has created. Board members rotate throughout the years, and staff members come and go. You need to ask if the organization will be able to manage your funds appropriately according to your original charitable intent.

"Some financial institutions have created reporting systems to help nonprofit organizations in their accountability to donors. They have systems that provide you with a statement on the value of your endowment fund as well as online access to view the value and activity of your fund at any time.

"These types of transparent reporting structures demonstrate the charity's desire to report to you the current results and status of your endowment fund. They also put in place an institutional memory that can keep a shifting administration accountable. Such consistent reporting makes it difficult for new board members and staff to change established disciplines."

As I watched him jiggle a purple jellybean from the box I said, "This brings up an interesting problem. Suppose I want to establish an endowment for an institution that clearly is not prepared to manage it. What then?"

"It's not really a problem," he said. "It's an opportunity. You can help them with your guidance as much as with your money. The way to do that is to create your own infrastructure. A friend from another accounting firm once told me a story of how a national civil rights leader did this.

"A donor came along who desired to create a large fund to benefit the cause the famous civil rights leader stood for. However, there was no management structure in place to properly handle the funds. Also, the civil rights leader wanted the donor to be comfortable in contributing such a large sum to benefit the cause. The solution was to find an attorney who could work with a local charitable consultant. Together they created an endowment fund to receive and administer the gift."

"How did that go for the civil rights cause?" I asked.

"Very well indeed," Mr. Howe replied. "They set up a fund and had it administered at a local financial institution which provided oversight to the foundation in the care and stewarding of the funds. In fact, in addition to the initial seed contribution, the fund received memorial gifts from donors all over the country when the leader passed away.

"The financial institution invested the fund and each year made distributions to the foundation to support its on-going programming in educating students about civil rights. The fund lasted for more than ten years.

"Because of the civil rights leader's wisdom in getting professional help, and foresight into what could be accomplished, that fund played a key role in sustaining the foundation's important mission.

"Great story, Mr. Howe," I responded. "How would you summarize what the civil rights leader did in terms of philanthropic planning strategies?"

Mr. Howe looked at me, replaced the package of jellybeans into his pocket, and quipped, "Sometimes, organizations simply do not have the kind of management structure they need to receive large gifts from donors.

"Using a charitable fund like the civil rights leader did with a third-party institution to assist in administration, you can create your own management structure that will give you the confidence and security you need to give all the money you want to any charity you want!"

I clapped him on the back and said, "Mr. Howe, you are reminding me of something I once heard Mr. Buffett say on a television interview. He said it is harder to give away money responsibly than it is to earn it."

"He should have come and talked to me," said Mr. Howe.

Chapter 18
An Unexpected Legacy

If I can establish my charitable foundation like Mr. Rockefeller, then maybe you can too! —Mr. EH

Back in the 20th floor conference room in the office building in downtown Detroit, I told Mr. Howe his donor contribution agreement was ready. When he signed, he would be creating the Eugene Howe Endowment Fund to support charitable organizations that help homeless persons become self-sufficient, independent, contributing members of society.

Mr. Howe continued to squint while looking up at me and said, "You have now heard all about my experiences and stories. You have a glimpse into my life and my thoughts, and maybe you can see why I came to ask you to set up my foundation like Mr. Rockefeller.

"Even though I plan to leave my money to my foundation upon death, I know that you will take care of everything for me the way that I want," he said. "By waiting until I die to fund my foundation, I feel better about maintaining flexibility to be able to change my mind about the details in the meantime."

I gave him a packet of information for his foundation including one of the signed copies of the agreement to take to his attorney, Mr. Spears. Mr.

Howe held open the left side of his coat, placed the packet of information into a large inside pocket, and strode off.

The following Thursday morning I received a phone call from Mr. Spears informing me that Mr. Howe had met with him that morning and handed over the packet of information. He said he would make sure Mr. Howe's estate was earmarked for distribution to his foundation upon his death. I drafted a note to the file describing my conversation with Mr. Spears and went about my business for the day.

Mr. Eugene Howe

One Thursday morning at 10 a.m., several years later, I received a call from Mr. Spears. "Eugene Howe passed away last week," he said. "I have a check for you in the amount of $170,000. Can you come to my office and sign the receipt for the distribution to his foundation?"

When Mr. Spears and I met, he told me, "Eugene will be very proud of what you have helped him to establish. As you know, during the later years of his life he lived on the streets of Detroit. He stored his personal belongings in an apartment located in the Cass Corridor, one of the roughest areas in the city. But he did not live there. He just stored his things there. He did not own a car, and he rode his bike everywhere, which is why he had a rubber band around one pant leg and a long white sock pulled up over the other pant leg."

Everyone on our streets knew Eugene. He was kind to all of us, and he had a heart of gold. He was always helping the people on the streets with whom he lived. He would help them to secure food, shelter, clothing, and even in locating a bathroom. He was also known to take someone who was having a terrible toothache to the dentist to help ease the pain.

One of the kindest and most thoughtful persons living on the streets of Detroit, Mr. Howe was also tough, and he had high expectations of those with whom he lived. He expected those who had received help from him to turn around and help others. He might encourage them to help someone find warm shelter, locate a shower, or discover a meal.

But, most importantly, Mr. Howe expected his fellow homeless persons to contribute to the good of the community. He encouraged them to help clean up a local park, street corner, or shelter after a good night of sleep. He insisted that they help both people and charitable organizations, always trying to identify those with the greatest needs.

"Yes, Eugene was a unique and special person," said Mr. Spears. "So it does not surprise me that he established his foundation like Mr. Rockefeller with all the possessions he owned on earth. His foundation will continue his legacy by generating $8,500 or more per year supporting charitable organizations and activities that assist homeless persons in becoming self-sufficient, independent, contributing members of society."

We shook hands. As we turned to walk our separate ways, Mr. Spears concluded, "You know, if Eugene Howe, who lived on the streets of Detroit, can establish his charitable foundation like Mr. Rockefeller, then maybe just about anyone can."

Chapter Notes

Chapter 1

"Eugene Howe Endowment Fund," *Community Foundation for Southeast Michigan Yearbook*, 1996.

Chapter 2

"John Davison Rockefeller, Sr.," *New York Times*, 24 May 1937.

Chapter 3

"How the world's wealth is distributed," by Mike Hanlon, *Gizmag*, 6 Dec. 2006.

"Giving USA 2013 Report," *Giving USA Foundation*.

"Charity and Motive: The Bequest Evidence from 17th-Century Wills" by Leslie McGranahan. Federal Reserve Bank of Chicago, Dec. 1998.

"Social Safety Net," Wikipedia, the Free Encyclopedia, Jan. 2014.

"U.S. Trust Study of High Net Worth Individuals and Professional Advisors," *Global Wealth and Investment Management*, Merrill Lynch, U.S. Trust, Bank of America, 2013.

"History of the Rockefeller Foundation," the Rockefeller Foundation Centennial project of the Rockefeller Archive Center (www.rockefeller100.org).

Thomas Ladenburg, Digitalhistory.uh.edu, 2007: 8.

[1]Allan Nevins, *John D. Rockefeller*, Volume I, p. 43, as cited in Raymond B. Fosdick, *The Story of the Rockefeller Foundation.* New York: Harper and Brothers, 1952: 4.

[2] Frederick T. Gates, *Chapters in My Life.* New York: The Free Press, 1977: 161.

[3] Fosdick 7.

[4] "General Education Board: Purpose and Program," Rockefeller Archive Center (RAC), Family Records, Rockefeller Boards, GEB, III 2 O, Box 15, Folder 145.

"Rockefeller Institute of Medical Research," Wikipedia, the Free Encyclopedia, May 2014.

"Biography: Ida Tarbell," American Experience Series, Public Broadcasting Station.

Chapter 4

"Giving USA 2013 Report," *Giving USA Foundation.*

Chapter 5

"Bill Gates and Bono on their Alliance of Fortune, Fame and Giving," *Forbes*, December 2, 2013.

"Howard Buffett: Farming and Finance," CBS News 60 Minutes, December 11, 2011.

The Salvation Army Ray and Joan Kroc Center San Diego, website, June 2014.

The Salvation Army National Office Marketing Department, May 2014.

Chapter 7

Emory University History: A Legacy of Heart and Mind: Emory Since 1836, by Gary S. Hauk.

Chapter 8

Survey of college pricing, The College Board, 2013-2014.

The Sudden Money Institute website, 2014.

"Albert C. Barnes," Wikipedia, the Free Encyclopedia, July 2014.

Chapter 9

History, Ford Foundation.org, July 2014.

History and Legacy, W.K. Kellogg Foundation.org, July 2014.

Chapter 10

Estate of Buck, Leagle.com, 2014.

Chapter 12

Interview with Bill Gates, *Forbes*, 19 May1997.

"For Wealth Holders: How much is enough? What you want your professional advisors to help you consider," Diana S. Newman, Philanthropic Consulting Group and Gregory A. Schupra, Comerica Charitable Services Group, 2002.

"Don't Eat the Chickens: Thoughts on Family Capital Preservation through Philanthropy," by Paul Comstock.

United States of America Census Bureau, 2010.

Chapter 14

"Population of the 20 largest U.S. Cities, 1900-2012, Infoplease website.

United States of America Census Bureau, 2010.

Historical Table 16, Nonprofit Charitable Organization and Domestic Private Foundation Information Returns, and Exempt Organization Business Income Tax Returns: Selected Financial Data, 1985 – 2010, Internal Revenue Service Statistics of Income Division, February 2014.

Robertson Lawsuit Background, Princeton University, January 2014.

Chapter 15

Donor's Estate Sues Metropolitan Opera, The New York Times, 24 July 2003.

Tennessee Division of the United Daughters of the Confederacy v. Vanderbilt University, Court of Appeals of Tennessee, 3 May 2005.

Chapter 16

SpringHill Camps website, October 2014.

Chapter 17

Uniform Law Commission: The National Conference of Commissioners on Uniform State Laws; Uniform Management of Institutional Funds Act (UMIFA) and Uniform Prudent Management of Institutional Funds Act (UPMIFA); Uniform Laws.org, 2014.

Acknowledgments

Philanthropy is a team sport. It requires many people performing their respective functions at a high level. This book is a testament to the professionalism of teammates I have worked with throughout the years. They pushed me to learn, grow, succeed at times, and fail at other times.

This book is also a tribute to the generous individual donors I have had the privilege of helping. Their generosity, like that of Mr. Eugene Howe, taught me about philanthropy and the real world.

In particular, I would like to thank Charles Bentzin for his mentorship and wisdom, and for allowing me to share here some of his philosophies and perspectives on giving.

This book would not have been possible without the able guidance of my publisher and friend Dr. Dan Runyon and his wife, Renée. I also want to thank the students in his 2014 Spring Arbor University copy editing class for their capable assistance.

Finally, I appreciate the encouragement of my awesome family: Brooke, Josh, Adler, and Kru Cole; Sara, David, and Mayes Van Winkle; and the love of my life, Ellie. For 35 years Ellie has been at my side, loving, encouraging, and prodding me to be the best person I can become in honoring God with my life.

To God be the glory!

G. A. Schupra

About the Author

For more than three decades, Mr. Gregory A. Schupra has educated and assisted thousands of people and their advisors in creating legacies leaving more than $1 billion of accumulated wealth to charity.

Mr. Schupra brings an uncommon and practical perspective to his work as a gift-planning professional by insuring that the philanthropic values, visions, and goals of donors align with their giving methods.

Often quoted by media sources on philanthropic issues, Mr. Schupra is frequently asked to present at professional advisor and donor education meetings, seminars, conferences, and workshops throughout the United States.

Mr. Schupra resides in Canton, Michigan, with his wife Ellie. They have two married daughters and three grandsons.

Made in the USA
Charleston, SC
07 March 2015